GERMANY'S SPIES AND SABOTEURS

D1365323

GERMANY'S SPIES AND SABOTEURS

DAVID ALAN JOHNSON

MBI Publishing Company

First published in 1998 by MBI Publishing Company, 729 Prospect Avenue, PO Box 1, Osceola, WI 54020-0001 USA

The information in this book is true and complete to the best of our knowledge. All recommendations are made without any guarantee on the part of the author or Publisher, who also disclaim any liability incurred in connection with the use of this data or specific details.

We recognize that some words, model names, and designations, for example, mentioned herein are the property of the trademark holder. We use them for identification purposes only. This is not an official publication.

MBI Publishing Company books are also available at discounts in bulk quantity for industrial or sales-promotional use. For details write to Special Sales Manager at Motorbooks International Wholesalers & Distributors, 729 Prospect Avenue, PO Box 1, Osceola, WI 54020-0001 USA.

Library of Congress Cataloging-in-Publication Data
Johnson, David Alan.
    Germany's spies & saboteurs: infiltrating the allies in World War II/ David Alan Johnson.
        p. cm.
    Includes index.
    ISBN 0-7603-0547-1 (alk. paper)
    1. World War, 1939–1945—Secret service—Germany. 2. Espionage, German—Great Britain. 3. Spies—Germany. 4. Irish Republican Army. I. Title.
D810.S7J585   1998
940.54'8743—dc21   98-7241

Printed in the United States of America

Contents

CHAPTER 1

Sabotage and Sedition

· · · · ·

To Lance Corporal Dieter Goeckel, the two old lifts symbolized not just the building, but the building's occupants as well. The lifts to the upper floors were impressively ornate, but they didn't work very often. Staff members and visitors frequently had to walk if they wanted to go upstairs; the two elevators were usually broken.

Lance Corporal Goeckel regularly drew guard duty at the building with the quaint old lifts: the headquarters of Germany's secret intelligence organization, the Abwehr, at 72-76 Tirpitz Ufer in Berlin. While on duty, he could observe both civilians and highly decorated officers of all the armed services as they came and went. "They knew how to put on a good show," he recalled, "but they never seemed to do very much."

Sometimes, a certain individual would report to Abwehr headquarters every day for weeks, and then suddenly disappear.

Rumors said that these unfortunates had been sent to the Russian front for failing in their jobs. Or, as Goeckel cynically suggested, "for failing to put the blame on somebody else."

During the course of the war, the Abwehr saw many of its agents vanish. Some were taken prisoner and quickly executed. Others returned to Berlin and were dispatched to less comfortable climates and assignments, as Goeckel had suggested. But many others remained under cover in enemy territory, sending intelligence reports back to Berlin or creating chaos with explosives and incendiary bombs.

But Lance Corporal Goeckel could be forgiven for coming away with the wrong impression of the Abwehr and its activities, since this was the impression that was intended. If Goeckel really wanted something or someone as a symbol of the organization, he should have chosen the Abwehr's director, Admiral Wilhelm Canaris. No man could have more completely symbolized an agency designed to confuse and deceive the enemy. Canaris was certainly a man of contradiction. No two people came away with the same impression of him, which was exactly the way Canaris wanted it.

He has been described as a "German patriot" as well as a "secret ally of the British." Although he once said that Adolf Hitler was "reasonable," Canaris would be executed in 1945 for suspected association with the plot to kill Hitler in July 1944. Prematurely gray, short of stature (about 5 feet 4 inches), and vague in manner, he did everything possible to give the impression of being incompetent, or at least not overly bright. A journalist who interviewed Canaris in 1935 wrote: "I could not believe that this rumpled, tongue-tied, simple-minded little man was the new chief of the Abwehr."

Canaris was anything but incompetent or simple-minded, however. During World War I, he had been an officer on the cruiser *Dresden* when it was caught by British cruisers off the Falkland Islands in 1915. The *Dresden* eventually sank off the coast of Chile, and the crew was interned by the Chilean authorities. Canaris, however, managed to escape interment. Two months later, he was back in Germany.

After the war, Canaris stayed in the navy. His right-wing views and his opinion favoring German rearmament earned him good reports from his superiors. By 1935, the year he became head of an unimportant espionage agency called the Abwehr, he was a captain. Later the same year, he was promoted to admiral.

Under Canaris, the Abwehr did not stay unimportant for very long. He supervised a complete transformation of the bureau. Within months after he became director, German agents began operating throughout Europe—especially in Poland, France, and the Netherlands—as well as in Africa, Japan, Britain, and the United States. Some of these people were quickly trained, and sometimes poorly, but they kept sending information back to the gray building on Tirpitz Ufer.

In Britain and the United States, the Abwehr had a network of sympathizers already in place before the war started. The United States had several pro-German and German-American organizations at work within its borders, ready to commit acts of espionage or sabotage on request. The best known of these groups was probably the German-American Bund. Active in both Britain and the United States was the Irish Republican Army.

The idea of recruiting the IRA against Britain was suggested by two Germans named Helmut Clissmann and Dr. Jupp Hoven, both of whom had spent long stays in Ireland in the 1920s and 1930s. Both would join the Abwehr when Germany and Britain went to war in 1939.

Helmut Clissman was on friendly terms with several prominent men within the IRA. The idea of an IRA/Abwehr collaboration, however, was not based solely upon Clissmann's friendships. It had more to do with an Irish bomb campaign in England during the early part of 1939.

The IRA began its bombing in January. It was an ambitious campaign, even by IRA standards. Power stations and other sites in London, Manchester, and Birmingham were blown up, as well as a power cable that ran above London's Grand Union Canal. About a month later, four London shops were set on fire. In March, a bomb exploded on Hammersmith Bridge in West London; it blew up supporting girders, snapped suspension cables, and dropped the entire bridge about a foot. Other bombs were exploded in King's Cross Railway Station and Victoria Station, as well as Southwark Power Station and several other places in London and other cities.

The reaction in London to all these explosions was alarm and outrage. The government responded by pronouncing that the Irish Republican Army did not exist. Berlin was quite impressed by all the chaos, however, almost in spite of itself. An editorial in the *Volkischer Beobachter* said, "The bomb attacks . . . demonstrate that the Irish Republicans are in earnest, for all their fantasy."

When German intelligence planners in Berlin discovered that the IRA had plans for more bombings in England, they were even more impressed. Helmut Clissmann and Dr. Jupp Hoven recommended that the IRA be put to use to further German ends. The man they spoke with was Colonel Erwin von Lahousen, the head of Abwehr II, the section whose specialty was sabotage and sedition.

After listening to Clissman and Dr. Hoven, and considering the damage already done by the Irish, Col. von Lahousen agreed that the IRA could certainly be very useful. The IRA had already demonstrated that it could strike anywhere in Britain, almost at will. If the bomb campaign continued, it would play hell with the British war effort. From Lahousen's position, the thing to do was to give the IRA as much German support as it needed. Even though Germany was not yet at war with the British, everyone knew that hostilities were not very far off.

An "Irish Section" was created within Abwehr II, and an officer was appointed to make contact with the Republicans. The Irish Section got in touch the IRA leaders that Dr. Hoven had mentioned; the IRA decided to send a man to Germany to talk about a mutually beneficial IRA/Abwehr connection.

The man they sent to Hamburg was Seamus O'Donovan, who was only a "part-time" member of the army by 1939. "Jim Donovan," as he was known, had been involved in IRA activities for most of his 40-odd years. His right hand was missing three of its fingers, a souvenir of an accident with a homemade bomb during the 1920s. With war between Germany and Britain fairly imminent, the IRA leadership sent him over to Germany to make contact with the Abwehr.

O' Donovan made three trips to Hamburg between February and August 1939. In Germany, he discussed the leadership and weaponry of the IRA. The Abwehr gave assurances of arms deliveries when war with Britain broke out. Contacts were another topic; a safe address for IRA visitors in London was exchanged, along with the address of an IRA-Abwehr courier in Brussels. The meetings were satisfactory for both sides—the Irish were to get money and weapons; in exchange, the Abwehr was to have a rash of bombings and destruction.

A few days after O'Donovan left Hamburg for the last time, Britain and Germany were at war. A code signal between Ireland and Germany was drafted, to be used in radio traffic between the two countries. It had to be done in haste; it was one item that had been forgotten during O'Donovan's visits. The code signal, which would verify the authenticity of a message between the IRA and Berlin, was "House of Parliament," a deliberate misspelling of "Houses of Parliament."

But the code phrase was not used for seven long weeks, while the Abwehr's Irish Section waited and fretted. Part of the difficulty was with the IRA radio transmitter, which was fairly weak and did not work all that well, and part was with a less than efficient radio operator.

On October 22, however, Berlin finally heard from its Irish radio contact. It came eight weeks after war had broken out and was only a request for weapons and equipment, the first of many. And, the Abwehr's war diary complained, the sender in Dublin's fair city did not even indicate "what supply route is now possible."

The communiqué may not have been as useful or as encouraging as Col. von Lahousen and his staff might have liked, but a communications link between the Abwehr and the Irish Republicans had been made at long last. This meant that the roughly 15,000 members of the IRA could now be contacted for sabotage or espionage assignments in England.

Actually, there had been a good many misgivings on both sides concerning the collaboration. Originally, any activities by Germany against Britain was out of the question. In *Mein Kampf,* Adolf Hitler declared Great Britain one of Germany's natural allies. (The other "natural ally" was Italy.) And when Canaris was given permission to begin secret operations against Britain in 1937, he was still not allowed to tamper with the Irish and their much-publicized neutrality.

Even after the war began, the IRA's pointless attacks on any target in England that seemed handy—including letter boxes and telephone coin boxes—gave Col. von Lahousen doubts. He wondered if the homicidal Republicans could be controlled. They were very good at blowing up cinemas, baggage rooms, and other unguarded objectives, but could they destroy factories and munitions plants?

The IRA had its dissenters, as well. Ireland was outspokenly sympathetic with Catholic Poland; Polish priests had been sent to concentration camps for refusing to preach Nazi doctrine at Mass. And when Hitler entered into a nonaggression pact with the Soviet Union, an atheistic country, IRA leaders were accused of having made "a pact with the Devil."

The Republicans were not pro-Nazi, however, or even pro-German, but they were fanatically anti-English. A well-known Irish saying, often heard during World War I, is "England's danger is Ireland's opportunity."

As far as the IRA leaders were concerned, they were not making any kind of an unholy alliance by joining forces with the Abwehr. The way they saw it, they were only using the Germans to meet their own ends—to drive England out of Northern Ireland and to bring about the unification of Ulster and the Republic of Ireland. They would do worse than make an alliance with the Nazis to keep their army supplied with money and weapons.

For the next several months, after the initial radio message, the Abwehr waited for further contact with the Republicans. One of the items on Col. von Lahousen's mind was the possibility of landing saboteurs in Ireland by U-Boat. But no word was forthcoming from his allies in the Emerald Isle.

During the third week of January 1940, Col. von Lahousen got the message he had been waiting for: The IRA finally had begun its work in England. They had blown up a major military target—the Royal Gunpowder Factory in Waltham Abbey, Essex, had been effectively destroyed by three massive explosions. Five people were killed, 30 injured, and the surrounding neighborhood had been damaged by the tremendous blasts.

Just as satisfying, the sabotage job also had a devastating effect upon British morale, as well as in the public's faith in Britain's counter-espionage system.

Actually, British counterintelligence (code named MI.5) got word of the impending Waltham Abbey sabotage long before Col. von Lahousen heard anything about it. In fact, MI.5 was fairly well informed of the coming event.

The head of MI.5 was Sir Vernon Kell. In the first days of 1940, Kell received an anonymous tip that the Royal Gunpowder Factory was to be the target of enemy sabotage. Kell assigned Chief Inspector William Salisbury to investigate. Inspector Salisbury was new to MI.5, but had been on Scotland Yard's murder squad for years and was well known for getting results.

Before Salisbury or his investigation could get anywhere, the IRA struck. The Royal Gunpowder Factory was destroyed on January 18.

Both Scotland Yard and MI.5 were at a complete loss concerning the explosions. Not only had they been unable to prevent the saboteurs from doing their job, in spite of being warned in advance, they were not even able to find out who the saboteurs were, in spite of Chief Inspector Salisbury and his famous Scotland Yard investigation methods.

News of the explosion came as a great shock to the British public. Only a few months before, in October 1939, the battleship *Royal Oak* had been sunk at its anchorage in Scapa Flow by a U-Boat. Rumors insisted that a German spy had guided the submarine into the anchorage. Now, a factory in a peaceful Essex town had been blown up by saboteurs.

A scapegoat was considered necessary to show the public that a "shakeup" in MI.5 was taking place. Prime Minister Neville Chamberlain demanded the resignation of MI.5's director, and Sir Vernon

Kell was thrown to the wolves to placate public opinion. In this case, they were Irish wolves.

Officially, the British government denied that the Waltham Abbey explosion, as well as every other act of sabotage during the war, was the result of enemy action. All were classified as "industrial accidents." But the firing of Vernon Kell is evidence that the government realized the truth.

Col. von Lahousen knew all about the explosions, as well as who caused them. The Abwehr's war diary refers to the saboteurs as "a group of Irish patriots with whom we are in contact."

The IRA had drawn up a "Sabotage plan," or "S-plan," which outlined the proposed bomb and propaganda campaign that was still to come. Among the places to be attacked were armament plants, transportation centers, gas works, power stations, industrial plants, and newspaper offices. To Col. von Lahousen, it looked as though the IRA's S-plan had got off to a flying start. Joining forces with the Republicans seemed to be one of the smartest moves the Abwehr had made in the young war.

In Dublin, the government of the Republic of Ireland were almost as alarmed over the IRA campaign as the British government. The Irish government was officially neutral—but unofficially very friendly with Germany—and did not want to antagonize either Britain or Germany. In fact, Ireland's president, Eamon de Valera, denied all accusations that saboteurs were using Ireland as a base for operations against England.

Actually, President de Valera's major worry was not what the IRA were doing in England. His main concern was over what the IRA might do in Ireland.

Nobody knew what the IRA was going to do, not even the leaders themselves; its members were split into factions and seldom agreed on anything. Although President de Valera was a former IRA member himself, he feared a strong army. Bolstered by money and weapons from the Germans, and huge sums of money from well-meaning contributors in the United States (who at least partially financed the bombings in England), he feared that the IRA might try to overthrow the government and install an army leader as the new president.

These fears were well founded. The IRA was certainly getting all it could out of the Abwehr. (Also out of private contributors in the

United States; one army member was arrested while carrying $7,500 in U.S. currency.) Money was sent to the IRA in Ireland and in England. Weapons and radio transmitters were dropped by parachute, or landed by U-Boat. The Abwehr's Irish Section sent $15,000 to the IRA through "Jim Donovan" in the spring of 1940. Other amounts, some considerably larger, were delivered to the Abwehr's Irish friends by agents.

Following the stunning success with the Royal Gunpowder Factory, however, the IRA was not doing very much to earn its money. At least this was Col. von Lahousen's opinion. His Irish friends were not performing the acts of sabotage they had promised, and for which they were being so well paid. Civilian targets were still being blown up with wild abandon—letter-boxes, baggage rooms, and the like—but no military objectives or war-production plants had been bombed for months.

Sometime in 1940, the head of the Irish Section, who used the cover name "Dr. Pfalzgraf," sent the following message to Ireland:

"The Pfalzgraf Section very urgently requests its Irish friends and IRA members to be so good as to carry out the S-plan . . . and to be more effective against military targets as opposed to civilian targets."

Col. von Lahousen even decided to use his own agents to work in Ireland. The plan was to send them into the country, where they would either work in collaboration with the IRA or, if the army decided not to go along, to wage their own sabotage campaign against the British. The Abwehr would communicate with these agents directly, instead of using IRA members as principal contacts.

It would have been a good plan if it had worked. But none of the men sent to Ireland by the Abwehr was able to offer very much help.

One agent was an Austrian named Ernst Weber-Drohl, who had toured Ireland as a professional circus performer before the war under the name "Atlas the Strong." Weber-Drohl landed by U-Boat in the early part of 1940, but was arrested for illegal entry shortly after wading ashore.

Col. von Lahousen tried again in May 1940. The Abwehr's man this time was Hermann Goertz, from Hamburg. Goertz's job was to bribe the IRA to blow up British shipping in Northern Ireland's harbors. He was supplied with a sizable lump of cash, with promises of more to come if the IRA did its job properly. With luck, the British might even be forced to divert troops to Northern Ireland to deal with the IRA and protect Ulster's ports and harbors.

But poor Herr Goertz had nothing but bad luck, from first to last. He was dropped in the wrong place, parachuted 70 miles away from his intended objective, and had to walk to his destination. Not the greatest of beginnings, and things got worse. When Goertz finally made contact with the IRA, the Republicans took all of his money and left him to be picked up by the police. He was arrested and interned for the duration of the war.

The Abwehr even tried to repatriate the IRA's former chief of staff, Sean Russell, who was fanatically anti-British. It was hoped that Russell would use his fiery manner, and his prestige within the army, to turn the IRA into a sabotage unit dedicated to creating havoc on a grand scale, both in England and as in Northern Ireland.

Sean Russell was in the United States in 1940. The Abwehr arranged his passage from New York to Genoa, then to Berlin for a briefing with Abwehr officers. He was not at all well; he suffered from stomach ulcers, among other things. In all probability, Russell should not have done any more traveling after arriving in Germany, at least not for a while. But he was eager to get back to Ireland, and Col. von Lahousen was anxious to have the IRA chief where he could be useful.

While on board the U-Boat that was to have landed him at Galway, Russell became violently ill and died, probably from a burst gastric ulcer. He was buried at sea, wrapped in the German naval ensign.

Because of bad luck or stupidity, or both, the Abwehr was not able to land any of its own men in Ireland. Canaris and Lahousen resigned themselves to the necessity of relying upon the IRA.

The Republicans were very good when they wanted to be, as they had already proved on several occasions, and they had contacts all over England. The main problem was that the army was split into several factions, including a Communist group and a "conservative" wing, who bitterly hated each other, and who used German weapons and equipment against each other. The Abwehr officers could see that one of their major obstacles was going to be convincing the IRA to fight the British instead of themselves.

There is a saying that bomb-throwing is the Irish version of original sin. Col. von Lahousen's task would be to get the IRA to throw its bombs in the right direction. The IRA leaders realized that they were going to have to cooperate with the Abwehr if they wanted German shipments of money and equipment to continue. Berlin was always after them to carry out the S-plan and hit military and industrial targets. Unless they did something to satisfy this request, the shipments from Germany, including all that money, would be cut off.

The IRA had the men and material to do the job.

Throughout Ireland, they had several "bomb schools"—classes for teaching the proper methods for making and handling bombs. Thanks to friends in the United States, besides payments from Berlin, the army had the funds to finance any operations in England. Rabid hatred of England had always been the IRA's motive.

Since the outbreak of the war in 1939, Berlin had supplied the army with money and supplies. Now the Abwehr was supplying an additional motive, as well.

Canaris employed the same basic methods against the United States as he had against Britain. At the start of the war, the Abwehr already had agents and saboteurs placed in strategic positions throughout the country. By the time the United States became an active belligerent, in December 1941, the U.S. would be covered by a network of German agents.

Irish Republican Army members were also used as agents in America by Col. von Lahousen. But the IRA was not the only group employed by the Abwehr. The sabotage and espionage organization within the United States was well planned; the network had been thought out long in advance.

In the East, spies had been planted at the docks where Allied shipping tied up, especially New York Harbor. Saboteurs were placed within the Harrison, New Jersey, gas works. Agents joined the staffs of numerous plants and factories to stage "accidents" and work slowdowns. Nazi sympathizers were situated in plants engaged in "essential war work," including Ford and Chrysler plants in Detroit, and the Bausch & Lomb factory in Rochester, New York, which made lenses for the Norden bomb sight.

A listing of important installations was drawn up—power stations, large factories, reservoirs, radio stations, and telephone exchanges. Americans of German ancestry were recruited to work for the Abwehr, to be planted inside the factories and power stations for the purpose of sabotage.

Inside Germany, a small group of specialists were being trained in the use of explosives. These were German citizens who had lived in the United States before the war and had an inside knowledge of the country and its ways. The Abwehr official in charge of this particular branch was Walter Kappe, who had lived in the United States from 1924 to 1937, and had been the press and propaganda director for the American edition of the Nazi party, the German-American Bund.

Sometimes, Canaris received help from naturalized Americans who had been born in Germany, legal citizens of the United States who still retained their loyalty to the old country. One such man was Herman Lang, an assembly inspector in the Norden plant in New York.

Herman Lang was not a spy, but he came in everyday contact with the drawings for the highly classified Norden bombsight, which was said to enable a bomb-aimer to hit a "pickle barrel" from thousands of feet above. Lang thought that Germany would do well to have such a sight, and he decided to do everything possible to help Germany build its own version of the fabled Norden sight.

Because of his job, Lang frequently was able to take one of the drawings home with him. At night, after his wife and family had gone to bed, he would make copies of the plans on tracing paper. In the morning, he would return the actual blueprint to the Norden plant.

Lang made contact with one of the Abwehr's many agents in the New York area. From this stage, it was fairly simple to smuggle the drawings out of the country. One of them was taken to Germany by a steward on the liner *Bremen,* rolled up in an umbrella.

The smuggled drawings allowed German engineers to make a working model of the Norden bomb sight, as well as to develop a supposedly improved version called the *Adler-Geraet* (Eagle Device). All of this happened in 1937. The Luftwaffe had the United States' "top secret" bomb sight two years before the war began, and four years before the United States formally entered the fighting. All through the efforts of a man who was not even an Abwehr employee.

The Irish Republican Army also served its purpose. IRA members were recruited for sabotage in the United States for the same reason that they were put to use in England—they knew how to handle explosives, they could move and strike at will, and were willing to do anything for money. They responded to the Abwehr's offer with enthusiasm. Any ally of the hated British was an enemy of the IRA. Especially if the IRA was being well paid.

An agent was sent directly to New York to negotiate with the IRA. The agent, Karl Rekowski, arrived carrying $200,000 for Col. von Lahousen's "Irish friends." This was a very large amount for the Abwehr to invest, but they were expecting big things in return.

Rekowski contacted the IRA leaders whom Berlin had indicated. (The same man who supplied Rekowski with the New York names and addresses had also made the arrangements between the IRA and Abwehr for operations against Britain.)

After negotiating with the Irish leaders, and showing at least part of the $200,000, Rekowski was able to assure Col. von Lahousen that the IRA had agreed to undertake sabotage on a substantial scale in the United States.

Among the targets on the IRA's list were: British ships in American harbors; warehouses stocked with supplies for the Allied war effort; lines of communication, including telephone exchanges; as well as any military or manufacturing centers deemed "essential." Rekowski also reported that the "Irish Nationalists," which they were usually called, had enough S-material on hand for the time being.

Col. von Lahousen's expectations seemed to have been well founded. On September 12, 1940, the IRA/Abwehr blew up the Hercules Powder Plant in Kenvil, New Jersey; the blast killed 52 people, caused millions of dollars worth of damage, and rattled windows for miles around. Two months later, on November 12, three war production plants, one in New Jersey and two in Pennsylvania, were also destroyed by spectacular explosions. Karl Rekowski was highly amused to read in the newspapers that Secretary of War Henry L. Stimson thought that the sabotage had been carried out with "Teutonic efficiency."

Most of the time, Rekowski stayed in Mexico to keep the Federal Bureau of Investigation from picking him up. One of his messages to Col. von Lahousen mentioned difficulties in getting explosives to his "northern friends." He asked if Berlin could possibly send instructions for the making of explosives and incendiary devices—it would simplify things if the IRA could make its own. (He also asked for a formula to make stink bombs, for disrupting political meetings.) And there were always requests for more money.

Apart from these items, Rekowski's reports were filled with encouraging news. Ships set on fire, trains derailed, factory machinery sabotaged. On March 9, 1941, he mentioned "17 steamers" successfully attacked. Sabotaging shipping was apparently a fairly simple matter. Security along the docks of New York and Boston was either lax or nonexistent, and quite a few of the dock workers were IRA members.

Although the IRA was working up to Col. von Lahousen's expectations, his "Irish friends" were not the only agents Abwehr II had in the United States. Another underground group that cooperated with Col. von Lahousen was a Ukrainian "revolutionary" organization that was dedicated to the overthrow of the Soviet government. This group was as enthusiastically pro-Nazi as it was anti-Soviet.

The head of the Ukrainians was Anastase Vonsiatsky, who called himself a "count" in order to marry a rich American. From his wife's vast estate in Connecticut, which was guarded by an army of security men and contained an arsenal of firearms and explosives, Vonsiatsky ran his organization in full cooperation with the Abwehr.

Any number of industrial "accidents" mysteriously occurred after Vonsiatsky met with an Abwehr representative in Chicago during December 1940. Not all of these can be attributed to the Ukrainian underground movement. But in April 1942, when the U.S. Navy was forced to take over the Brewster Aeronautical Company because the plant had not delivered a single aircraft to the U.S. armed forces, the Abwehr was found to have had 32 of its agents installed in the factory. At least two were Ukrainians; the rest were with the German-American Bund or were pro-Nazi in sympathy. When these people were removed from the factory, the delivery schedule returned to normal.

A similar occurrence took place at the Liquidometer plant in New York, which manufactured pipes and tubing for ships and aircraft. The factory suffered from a rash of accidents and slowdowns until a suspect department supervisor, a machinist, and a foreman were dismissed. It had been discovered that all three men were actively pro-Nazi.

Throughout 1940 and 1941, the Hartford Fire Insurance Company recorded 40 "mysterious" fires and explosions. Most occurred in the eastern part of the United States, although one happened in Wisconsin and another at an Army barracks at Fort McDowell, near

San Francisco. All involved ships and facilities belonging either to Britain or France, U.S. government munitions factories, or war-related industry. The Navy Department building in Washington, D.C., also mysteriously caught fire. All fires and explosions were listed as being "of unknown origin."

The Federal Bureau of Investigation denied that any of these incidents were the result of sabotage, just as Scotland Yard and MI.5 had done. According to an "official" history of the FBI, "The suspected sabotage cases were, for the most part, industrial accidents caused by fatigue, carelessness, spite, a momentary burst of anger, or horseplay among the workers."

It was going to be a long and frustrating war for the FBI, as well as for Scotland Yard and British counterintelligence, compliments of Col. von Lahousen, Canaris, and their various 'friends" on both sides of the Atlantic.

CHAPTER 2

Operation Pastorius

• • • • •

C ANARIS COULD WELL AFFORD TO BE SATISFIED. HIS ESPIONAGE AND SABO-
tage agents in Britain and the United States were doing an excellent job, successfully creating chaos for the enemy as well as sending
intelligence reports back to Berlin. There had been a few setbacks,
notably with the plan to plant Abwehr agents in Ireland, but he was
generally optimistic about future operations in both countries.

The admiral was especially happy with the way things were
turning out in the United States. He had the contacts and resources
inside the United States that allowed the Abwehr access to military
bases, important installations, port facilities, and industrial plants
throughout the country. Besides setting fires and planting bombs,
the Abwehr's pro-Nazis, "good Germans," and paid agents were
sending a steady flow of "classified" information to headquarters.
Messages regarding convoys' departures from Eastern ports—dates
of sailing and numbers of ships—as well as the number of B-17 Flying Fortresses being sent to Britain, and technical details of aircraft
and warships were regularly dispatched to Tirpitz Ufer.

Still, some objectives were considered too important to be left
to amateurs—enthusiastic amateurs, to be sure, but still amateurs. One of the most important of these objectives was the Aluminum Company of America and its three factories, which were
vital to the U.S. aircraft industry and were already marked as targets for saboteurs. The Abwehr had diagrams of all three of the
company's plants: at Alice, Tennessee; Massena, New York; and
East St. Louis, Illinois—all courtesy of German agents inside the
United States.

Another major concern was American coal production. Canaris
and Col. von Lahousen were particularly interested in crippling the

rail transport system between the coal mines in Pennsylvania and West Virginia and the Pittsburgh steel mills.

The Chesapeake and Ohio Railroad, which carried most of the coal, was a particularly attractive target. The railway's "horseshoe curve" at Altoona, Pennsylvania, was known to be a bottleneck—once again, thanks to the Abwehr's agents. If the horseshoe curve were blown up, delivery of coal would suffer for quite some time, along with production of steel.

Col. von Lahousen insisted that the orders to blow up these objectives had come from Adolf Hitler himself. Wherever the original idea came from, its first stages went into motion shortly after the United States and Germany went to war in December 1941.

Once the idea of the sabotage operation had officially been accepted, a plan had to be drawn up to breathe life into it. Col. von Lahousen named Walter Kappe, the former German-American Bund director of press and propaganda, to find the men who would carry out the operation, as well as to oversee their intensive training.

Walter Kappe was far from the best man for the job. The fact that Kappe was entrusted with such an assignment in the first place had more to do with his abilities in salesmanship and self-promotion than his skills in managing and organizing.

Kappe had always fancied himself as having more talent and ability than he actually possessed, and he had the knack of convincing others of the same thing.

Kappe had the ability to talk his way into any job or situation he wanted. His background was not very impressive; he was a university drop-out who spent most of his working life in factories. But in 1925, about a year after he left Germany and came to the United States, Kappe applied for a job as a reporter with the German-language Chicago *Abendpost*. Even though he had no qualifications to be a reporter, his gifts for talking and selling himself apparently impressed the managing editor; Kappe got the job.

Kappe talked himself into a number of good jobs. He rose from reporter to editor. As editor of the German-American Bund newspaper *Deutcher Weckruf und Beobachter*, he was able to dictate his own editorial policy. When he returned to Germany in 1937, after 13 years in the United States, the stocky 32-year-old used his talent for talk, and his Bund connections, to land another prize. By making more of his experiences in the United States than the truth would support, he received an appointment as propaganda head of Berlin radio station DJB, which broadcast to both North and South America.

In September 1939, war finally broke out. Kappe was stationed on the French frontier and saw service in the Wehrmacht—as an officer. But in 1941, when Berlin's watchful eyes began paying increased attention to the United States, Kappe was transferred to the Abwehr.

Kappe's inflated account of his accomplishments in the United States had come to the attention of Col. von Lahousen. On the strength of this record, and on Kappe's gift for gab, he was placed in charge of a section of Berlin's Ausland Institut. His job was to update data that the Abwehr had on file regarding Germans who had lived in the United States, and to interview repatriated Germans who might prove useful in some future capacity. He worked out of an office at Number 8 Rankestrasse, which was disguised as the editorial office of a nonexistent magazine called *Der Kaukasus*.

Kappe was more than satisfied with himself for having secured his position at the Ausland Institut. He was convinced that he had finally found a job worthy of his superior talents. And later in the year, when Col. von Lahousen gave him the job of overseeing a major sabotage operation in America, it came as no surprise to him. Kappe reasoned that his ability and intelligence were being given their due recognition.

He threw himself into the assignment. He studied the American coal and light metal industries. He read recent field reports sent by agents in the United States, especially the updated information on the plants and railway lines to be destroyed. He sifted through the records of every potential saboteur, and traveled throughout Germany to talk to them.

Kappe also thought up a name for the operation. In an attempt at sarcastic humor, he called it "Operation Pastorius," after the first German immigrant to land in America, in 1683, one Franz Daniel Pastorius.

Most of the people interviewed for Operation Pastorius were found to be unacceptable by Knappe. Some spoke little or no English, despite having lived in the United States for many years. They had never traveled outside their small German-American communities and had no idea how most Americans lived and behaved. They would have been spotted as aliens and arrested before they could get anywhere near their objective.

Some of the interviewees could speak the language like those born and reared in America, and knew all about baseball and other American customs, but turned out to be nervous and highly strung, which made them temperamentally unfit to take part in anything as risky as a sabotage operation.

The job of finding likely candidates turned out to be a lot more difficult than Kappe expected, but he finally managed to find 12 people who met all his qualifications. Further screening eliminated four of the original men, but eight men would be enough to do the job, Kappe decided, if they were properly trained. At long last, Operation Pastorius was ready to be launched.

According to the plan, the operation would be divided into two phases. The eight men were to be split into two groups of four. Each of the groups would land at a different place along the Atlantic coast, to make detection more difficult for the U.S. authorities.

From what Kappe knew of them, all eight of the final candidates seemed to be ideally suited for the sabotage operation. All were young and fit, ranging in age from 22 years to 39 years. Each of them had lived in the United States for many years; spoke the language fluently, if with an accent; and were at home with Americans and their ways. They should have no trouble blending with the country and its people. The leaders of the two groups were George Dasch and Edward Kerling, chosen by Kappe because they were both thorough, capable, and able to take orders from Kappe.

Because of the quality of the men, the intensive training that the eight of them were about to undergo, and the Abwehr's well-established contacts inside the United States, there was no doubt in Kappe's mind that Operation Pastorius would succeed. With this triumph under his belt, there was no telling what sort of reward would be in store for him. He would get a promotion, at least. Maybe even a medal.

But Kappe should have been more thorough in screening his candidates. One of the leaders of the two sabotage groups, George Dasch, was not the man Walter Kappe thought him to be. Dasch was a non-Nazi who became an anti-Nazi. He was also a repatriated German citizen who regretted that he ever came back to Germany.

The only reason that George Dasch ever returned to Germany at all, after 19 years in the United States, was that his mother talked him into it. Dasch had been working as a waiter, a job he was not entirely happy with. When his mother came from Germany to visit him in 1939, she was not very happy, either, when she found out that her son was only a waiter. She advised him to go back to Germany, where he would be able to get a much better job. Her brother Adolf was a senior employee with the huge chemical conglomerate I. G. Farben, and she was sure that George's Uncle Adolf could get him a good position in the same firm.

It was a crack-brained and impulsive thing for Dasch ever to have listened to such an idea. For one thing, he was married to an American girl, Rose Marie Guilli, to whom he gave the affectionate and slightly silly name "Snooks." For another, Dasch was anything but sympathetic to the Nazi cause—he and other members of his waiters' union used to harass German-American Bund meetings whenever the opportunity presented itself.

But once Dasch got an idea into his head, nothing would dislodge it. The only way for him to get to Germany from New York, because of the war, was by way of Japan, China, and through Soviet Russia, which took seven weeks. But he was determined and endured the trip. And when he finally arrived, in May 1941, his mother told him that his coming was a mistake—she said that he never should have left the United States.

Dasch first met Walter Kappe while he was being interviewed by immigration officials. Kappe tried to talk him out of going to work for I. G. Farben and did his best to recruit Dasch "for the little political system he was always building up." Dasch indicated that he was going to visit his mother before he did anything else. Kappe told him to come and see him in Berlin after his visit, and handed him a card with the Rankestrasse 8 address.

Dasch had no real intention of taking Kappe up on his offer. Besides, he had a more urgent matter on his mind—his wife had not been heard from in over six weeks, ever since she left New York to join Dasch in Germany. She left in late April, aboard the Spanish liner *Marquise de Camille*, but the ship never reached Spain.

In an effort to find out what happened to his wife, Dasch cut his visit to his mother short and went to Berlin. He hoped that he might learn something after making inquiries among government agencies, and Berlin was the logical place to start.

He was not able to learn anything. For several days, he was passed from office to office; nobody seemed to know or care anything about his problem. Eventually, he was directed to the office of—Walter Kappe. Herr Kappe had connections in official circles and, Dasch was told, might be able to help him out.

Kappe had enough influence to find out the whereabouts of Dasch's wife with very little effort. The Foreign Office informed Dasch that the *Marquise de Camille* had been stopped en route to Spain by British warships, and that his wife had been removed to Bermuda. She would be interned in Bermuda, he was told, for the duration of the war.

Dasch was relieved to hear that his wife was safe, although disappointed that he would not be able to see her for several years. But, he reasoned, it was just as well that she could not come to Germany. With her outspoken manner, she would be almost certain to get herself in trouble with the Nazi regime at some point in time.

Once this little errand had been tended to, Kappe once again tried to recruit Dasch into his sphere of influence. He even took Dasch to lunch, where he could continue his line of persuasion under more agreeable surroundings.

In spite of Dasch's determination to work for I. G. Farben, Kappe's line of gab impressed him. Kappe promised to get Dasch a job as an *erfasser*, a radio monitor, translating American news broadcasts for government officials. This position, he insisted, would make the most of Dasch's American background and command of the "American" language.

But even more impressive, as far as Dasch was concerned, were the benefits that went with the job—exemption from military service, a room in one of Berlin's more exclusive boarding houses with ration-free dining, and the chance to buy whiskey and other scarce items, as well as a number of other privileges.

After listening to Kappe's hard sell, Dasch was convinced that his best interests lay in working for the government. He forgot all about I. G. Farben and was soon translating American radio broadcasts at Berlin's Seehaus.

But Dasch was already beginning to think that his returning to Germany had been a mistake, as his mother had said. Life in Nazi Germany was too restricting for him, especially after 19 years in the

United States. The country was far from the place he had known as a teenager. The Gestapo were always checking up on him, for evidence of "treasonable" activities, and the police were everywhere, looking for an excuse to start trouble.

Because of government restrictions, however, and the war, there was no way for him to get out of Germany, as much as he would have liked to return to America. His dislike of the "damned Nazis" quickly turned to contempt.

One of the many things that irritated Dasch was the strict censorship on all news releases. The only stories passed by the official censors were propaganda pieces, which glorified the Nazi regime in general and Adolf Hitler in particular. He had the chance to hear other views of the war, because of his job monitoring American news items, and he wished that he could release the contents of the American broadcasts to the German public.

He had been at the Seehaus only a short time when he got his wish. Dasch's views on the Nazi party became known to one of his fellow workers, a Fraulein Piper. Fraulein Piper agreed with his opinion and introduced him to others who had no use for the Nazis. Dasch was surprised to find that a secret anti-Nazi underground network was operating right in Berlin.

One activity of this secret group was to smuggle copies of the secret *Funkspiel*, the daily uncensored news broadcasts from the United States, out of the building. Stories from the stolen news reports were run off on a small printing press and mimeograph machine. These highly illegal "newspapers" were distributed all over Germany, at great risk.

Outside the secret anti-Nazi society, Dasch was very careful about expressing his views of Hitler and his party. The Gestapo were constantly nosing around the Seehaus, making sure that the staff remained loyal party members. His landlady at the boarding house was also a Gestapo informer, along with several of Dasch's fellow tenants. To keep the Gestapo from getting suspicious, Dasch made a special effort to play the part of the loyal Nazi. Whenever his landlady was within hearing, he would loudly complain about wanting to fight for Hitler instead of remaining a useless civilian.

At the same time, he kept trying to get out of Germany. He applied for posts as a radio monitor in Paris and in Bucharest, but both applications were turned down.

His landlady overheard Dasch's talk about wanting to fight for Hitler, as he had planned. One day, one of his landlady's visitors heard him, as well. Through this visitor, a young woman who held some mysterious post in the government, Dasch was summoned to meet a man attached to the Abwehr.

A few days after this meeting, which was held in secret and was very perplexing to Dasch, he received another summons. He was to meet with Walter Kappe at the Wehrmacht High Command Building.

Dasch was surprised to hear from Walter Kappe again. He was even more surprised when Kappe questioned him about ports and harbors along the Atlantic coast of the United States and about making a landing in America. Germany was not yet at war with the United States. Dasch could only guess at what Kappe and the Abwehr wanted.

Japan propelled the United States into the war with the surprise air attack on the American fleet at Pearl Harbor, Hawaii, on December 7, 1941. Four days later, Adolf Hitler declared war on the United States. With Hitler's declaration, Kappe intensified his interrogation of George Dasch.

Dasch was routinely questioned about his life history and his experiences in the United States—the Abwehr was testing to find if he was telling the truth, trying to catch him out on any irregularities in his story. Dasch realized that he was under close scrutiny, by the Gestapo as well as by the Abwehr, but still had no real idea what was behind in all. Kappe mentioned sabotage on one occasion, which gave Dasch his first clue. But aside from this, he had very little to go on.

At long last, Col. von Lahousen thought it was time to tell Dasch about the job he had been chosen for. At Kappe's Rankestrasse office, Dasch was informed that the High Command was planning a sabotage operation against the light metals and coal industries inside the United States. He was also told that he had been named to lead one of the sabotage teams that would land on the American coast.

Dasch faced a dilemma. There was no way in which he could back out of the operation—if he refused to go, he would be putting not only his own life in jeopardy, but also the lives of his mother and other relatives inside Germany. But at the same time, he knew that he would not be able to go through with his assignment to blow up American factories.

Because he had spent most of his adult life in the United States, including a brief stint in the U.S. Army in 1927–1928, Dasch considered himself an American citizen; he had passed his citizenship test in 1939 but, since he had already decided to return to Germany by then, he never showed up for his final swearing in as a naturalized American. More than ever, he now regretted ever having left the United States in the first place.

It was much too late for any second thoughts at this stage, however. Operation Pastorius had already gone past the preliminary stage, and he was part of it, whether he liked it or not.

At the end of February 1942, Dasch was formally transferred from the Foreign Office, and his job as a radio monitor at the Seehaus, to the Abwehr. He was also given the pseudonym "Strich"—a Strich being German for "dash" or hyphen. Another Abwehr attempt at humor.

In preparation for the operation, Dasch was required to attend any number of meetings and planning sessions, most of which were presided over by Col. von Lahousen. Every point of the coming landing was talked over in minute detail. The amount of money to be carried by the saboteurs was one of the topics under discussion. It was decided that $150,000 would be taken along for expenses and any necessary bribes.

Contacts with Abwehr agents inside the United States were also mentioned. The Nazis had sympathizers and paid agents in nearly every industrial center within the United States.

Another point of discussion was whether or not the saboteurs should carry firearms. It was suggested that each man carry a Walther semi-automatic pistol. Dasch vetoed this idea. He was afraid that one of the men might panic and kill a policeman, which would add "all kinds of complications" to his scheme for scuttling the operation. The idea was finally dropped, but not before Dasch endured a lot of angry arguments—the senior Abwehr officers did not take kindly to being contradicted.

Dasch had already decided to do something that would make the operation fail, but he did not know what. He had no intention of helping the Nazis inflict an act of sabotage against his adopted country.

But everything had been so carefully planned that the operation seemed certain to succeed. The "Pastorius team" had even been split into groups—if Dasch were able to stop his own group somehow, the other four men would still reach their objectives. "The whole thing," Dasch remarked, "was very thoroughly and carefully plotted in the best German tradition."

Dasch had a scheme to send a letter to the U.S. Embassy in Bern, Switzerland, in which he would outline the objectives of Operation Pastorius. His mother was going to Switzerland in February 1942. He planned to ask his mother to smuggle the letter out of Germany with her.

He did not sign his name to the letter; instead, he gave his serial number, 6-693-731, which he had been given by the U.S. Army 15 years before. But his mother refused to go along with the idea. She was afraid that the Gestapo would somehow find out about what she had done, and she decided that it was too risky for herself and her family.

One of Dasch's main worries was his own temperament. He was nervous and highly excitable, and he feared that he might do something while under stress that would give him away. Or, in his own words, "blow my stack and get tossed into a concentration camp."

The men chosen for Operation Pastorius, including Dasch himself, were due to begin their intensified training in sabotage and subversion fairly soon—sometime during the spring of 1942. The landings themselves would take place very shortly after their crash course had finished. If the operation was ever to be stopped, Dasch would have to think of some way of doing it before he and the other seven men left Germany. Or at least before they reached the United States.

Thirty five hundred miles west of Berlin, in Washington, D.C., the director of the Federal Bureau of Investigation had no inkling whatever that Operation Pastorius was about to be launched. Which was not surprising, considering J. Edgar Hoover's record against enemy spies and saboteurs. Although the FBI had been able to apprehend quite a few of the Abwehr's agents since war had broken out in Europe in 1939, most of these captures were made either because of luck or because one of the Abwehr's agents turned himself over to the bureau.

The FBI's greatest success had been the "Sebold affair." It involved a German named Wilhelm George Debowski, who came to the United States in the 1920s and "Americanized" his name to William G. Sebold.

Mr. Sebold decided to return to Germany in 1939 to visit relatives. The Abwehr was informed of his arrival, along with the fact that Sebold had worked as a mechanic for the Consolidated Aircraft Corporation in California. Col. von Lahousen's men tried to recruit him for "undercover work" in the United States.

Sebold wanted no part of the Abwehr or their scheme, however. So the Abwehr resorted to blackmail to secure his services. While checking into Sebold's background, someone had discovered that he had spent time in a German jail for smuggling. The Abwehr also found out that Sebold had failed to mention this conviction when he applied for American citizenship.

After Sebold had turned down the Abwehr twice, they offered him an alternative: either he would go to work for them, or they would inform the American authorities of his criminal record. In addition, he would not be allowed to leave Germany and would be sent to a concentration camp. Sebold agreed to the Abwehr's proposition.

Before sending Sebold back to the United States, the Abwehr trained him in the methods of microphotography, coding and decoding messages, and operating a radio transmitter. They also gave Sebold a false American passport, as well as the names of several reliable contacts in New York.

He arrived in New York City in February 1940 and immediately set up his secret radio transmitter. But before he did anything, he went straight to the FBI and told them everything. From the first, Sebold was never an Abwehr agent, but an informer for the FBI.

Because of Sebold, the FBI was able to learn many vital details about the German spy network in the New York area. For 16 months, from February 1940 to June 1941, the FBI used Sebold's short-wave set on Long Island to find out about the espionage operation. In exchange, they sent inaccurate and totally useless information about American defense plants and shipping movements. In June, the FBI thought it was about time to strike; they arrested numerous German agents and accomplices for espionage.

J. Edgar Hoover used the "Sebold incident" to his own advantage. With Hoover's prompting, newspapers ran banner headlines about how the FBI and its director had cracked the big Nazi spy ring. Radio broadcasts also played the story up big, giving the impression that Hoover had done the job all by himself.

Had it not been for Sebold, however, the FBI never would have known the whereabouts of the Abwehr's agents. And despite Sebold's revelations, German agents still operated in the United States on an extensive scale, in spite of Hoover's claims to the contrary. The FBI had been lucky, but the Abwehr were not so easily discouraged, or put out of work.

Hoover's methods lent themselves more to publicity than efficiency—successful captures of "enemy agents" were blasted across every front page in the country, but the bureau's failures were buried under strict security.

If George Dasch was counting upon J. Edgar Hoover and his bureau to help him foil Operation Pastorius, he was indulging in a pipe dream. With Hoover directing the FBI, the Abwehr enjoyed several spectacular successes in the United States, including the Hercules Powder Plant explosion. (Which had taken place while the FBI was monitoring Abwehr activities via Sebold's short wave set, in September 1940.) His ineffectiveness would do the same for the Pastorius mission.

William Colepaugh, an American citizen born in Connecticut, managed to make his way to Germany in 1943. He wanted to join the Wehrmacht but, for a number of reasons—especially his inability to speak German—was rejected. Instead, he was assigned to the SS Intelligence service, where his American English might prove useful. Although he was given a thorough training course in sabotage for an operation in the United States, he proved to be temperamentally unfit for such a secret operation.

Erich Gimpel had worked as an agent in Peru for several years before being chosen for a sabotage job in the United States. His background in espionage, and his accelerated "spy course" in Germany, made Gimpel an excellent choice for such an operation. But because he knew almost nothing of the country, he would need a reliable partner who was thoroughly familiar with America and its customs.

The conditions of traveling by U-Boat, cramped quarters, foul air, taut nerves, and tensions, are evident from this photo of a German submarine crew on an Atlantic patrol. The U-Boat was the main transport for German spies landing in the United States, but traveling by submarine was not a pleasant experience. The Abwehr agents and their equipment were crammed into the small boat, and the passengers endured a cooped-up, and frequently seasick, Atlantic crossing.

A U-Boat prepares to enter one of the submarine pens at Lorient, on the Bay of Biscay coast. The roofs of these pens were solid concrete, several feet thick, which made them all but impervious to British and American bombs. Lorient was one of the main U-Boat bases for operations against British and American shipping in the Atlantic. It was also the port of departure for George Dasch and his group in *U-202*, the group that would land on Long Island. The other four men, who sailed for Florida aboard *U-584*, departed from Brest.

Left and below
The Norden bomb sight, which was said to give American bombardiers the ability to hit a pinpoint target from thousands of feet above, was also one of the most strictly guarded secrets of the war. It was not even allowed to appear in news photos. Actually, Germany already had the drawings for the "top secret" bomb sight. They were copied by Hermann Lang, an assembly inspector at the Norden plant in New York, and smuggled to Germany in 1937. These drawings were used to make a working model of the bomb sight by technicians inside Germany. This unusual photograph of Hermann Lang was taken by a concealed FBI camera in New York, some time after he had sent the Norden drawings out of the country.

One of Nazi Germany's most ardent supporters in South America was General Edelmiro J. Farrell (Left) . General Farrell assumed the presidency of Argentina in February 1944, when he forced the resignation of President Pedro Ramirez (Right). President Ramirez and his government had planned to declare war on Germany and Japan. But General Farrell and the powerful clique of army colonels were actively pro-German; they had accepted German military assistance and, in return, allowed German agents to operate in Argentina without interference. President Ramirez's resignation, and General Farrell's rise to power, would prove a great benefit to the Abwehr. It would also be a major setback for Britain and the United States in their battle to stop German espionage in South America.

The eight men assigned to Operation Pastorius. Upper row: George Dasch, Ernst Peter Burger, Richard Quirin, Heinrich Heinck. Bottom row: Edward Kerling, Herbert Haupt, Werner Thiel, and Hermann Neubauer. Edward Kerling was in charge of the four-man team that landed in Ponte Vedra, Florida. George Dasch led the Long Island group. According to the original plan, the operation was to have included twelve men. But the four men not pictured were removed from Operation Pastorius, each for a separate reason.

A major focus of attention for German agents in Britain was the buildup of American air power. Members of the Irish Republican Army reported on the movement of U.S. bombers in Northern Ireland—their arrival from America, and their departure for U.S. Eighth Air Force bases in England. In Northern Ireland, as well as England, anyone could approach the boundaries of an American air base, on foot or on a bicycle, and watch the Flying Fortresses (or Liberators) come and go. German agents did their share of watching, and sent reports of what they had observed to Germany.

Reichsmarschall Hermann Göring was vitally interested in reports on both British and American air strength in the British Isles. During the buildup of the Eighth Air Force in 1942 and 1943, information on American bomber and fighter units—including identification numbers, location of bases, and commanding officer—were regularly received by Luftwaffe Intelligence.

Feldmarschall Erwin Rommel, the "Desert Fox," owed a measure of his legendary success to reports supplied by German Intelligence. In tank battles fought during the Libyan campaign, his Afrika Korps enjoyed the benefit of classified reports on British armored units and equipment. Similar information was also of no small assistance during the six-week Blitzkrieg in May and June 1940, when German Panzer forces swept through France and the Low Countries. Agents in Britain kept the Wehrmacht well advised of British tanks and their strengths and weaknesses.

At the Atlantic Charter meeting in August 1941, on board the battleship H.M.S. *Prince of Wales*, Prime Minister Winston Churchill hand-delivers a letter from George VI to President Franklin D. Roosevelt. A little over a year earlier, this would have been the only safe method of communication between the two. A member of the U.S. Embassy staff in London, named Tyler Kent, had intercepted messages between Churchill and Roosevelt; these were then passed along to an acquaintance, who passed them along to Berlin. The German government was kept well informed of Churchill's secret attempts to enlist the United States as an ally against Germany, and plans for American aid to Britain was also furnished with other highly classified military information.

The end of a German spy, at the hands of a U.S. Army firing squad. Most spies were not executed, however, but were "turned"—given the option of working for British or American Intelligence instead of facing the hangman. As double-agents, these turned spies sent authentic-sounding but inaccurate information to Berlin. But some of these "turned" agents managed to send bits of genuine information buried inside their false reports—bits that were called "flowers." And so, they managed to keep Germany abreast of British and American plans throughout the war, in spite of their supposed captivity.

39

A Type VII-C U-Boat, the same type as *U-202* and *U-584*. The U-Boat was one of the prime beneficiaries of the Abwehr and its activities. Submarine crews made full use of information gathered by the Abwehr. Agents in the United States, Britain, and South America sent a steady stream of information on Allied shipping and on convoy movements.

Admiral Karl Donitz, commander of U-Boat operations. He did not like Admiral Wilhelm Canaris, the Abwehr's chief, very much, and is said to have resented the use of his U-Boats to transport spies and saboteurs. But he realized that the submarine fleet depended heavily upon information sent by agents in the United States and the British Isles, as well as South America. Spies in these countries were an enormous help to U-Boat captains in reporting Allied shipping and convoy movements.

As commander-in-chief of U.S. forces, President Franklin D. Roosevelt had the power to authorize a military tribunal for George Dasch and the other Operation Pastorius defendants. Trying civilians by military law was legal. There was even a precedent—in 1865, the conspirators in Abraham Lincoln's assassination were tried by military tribunal. But the decision was highly unusual and controversial; under military law, the accused is presumed guilty until proven innocent.

Admiral Wilhelm Canaris was appointed chief of the Abwehr, Nazi Germany's intelligence agency, in 1935. The Abwehr was established in 1933, shortly after Adolf Hitler and the Nazis came to power. Under Canaris' direction, it became one of the world's leading espionage and sabotage organizations. The Abwehr had agents throughout Europe and Asia, as well as in North America and South America, sending a steady stream of useful information back to Germany. Although short of stature and not very impressive in his appearance, Adm. Canaris was deceptively sharp-witted and able. As early as 1939, before most senior German officers even began thinking about America or American intervention, he foresaw the entry of the United States into the war as an ally of Britain. In spite of his dedication to the Abwehr and its efficiency, Canaris was no friend to either Adolf Hitler or his regime. He was implicated in the assassination plot to kill Hitler on July 20, 1944, and hanged on April 9, 1945.

Kapitanleutnant Gunter Prien, captain of *U-47*, (left) is congratulated after returning from another successful Atlantic patrol. Prien and his fellow submarine commanders took a dreadful toll on British and American shipping during the early part of the war. Throughout 1940 and 1941 shipping losses continued at an alarming rate. These losses were due in large measure to reports from German agents in South America and in East Coast ports of the United States. Informers sent word of departing convoys to Germany. Admiral Dönitz, commander of the U-Boat fleet, passed this information along to his submarines at sea. Captains of individual U-Boats, including Bunter Prien, could then determine the best course to intercept and attack the convoy.

Although Johan Siegfried Becker was not an employee of the Abwehr, he organized and directed German espionage in Argentina after 1942. Becker's spy activities were carried out with the full cooperation of the ruling military government, including Juan Peron. In an attempt to end this official protection of German agents, the United States brought economic pressure to bear against Argentina. These economic sanctions had little effect, however. Becker and his contacts kept sending reports to Germany throughout the war.

The Cunard luxury liner *Queen Elizabeth* was converted into a troop transport, and carried thousands of men in a single crossing. She did not sail in a convoy, but relied upon her speed to outrun U-Boats and their torpedoes. Although spies in Britain and in South America kept a steady eye out for the *Queen*, and kept Germany well informed of her movements, she managed to evade German submarines over numerous Atlantic crossings.

The German High Command knew that the Allied forces would land an amphibious force somewhere on the northern coast of France. But the question was: When would the invasion take place, and on what part of the French coast? Agents in Britain sent a steady stream of reports regarding the build-up of Allied troops—infantry, armor, paratroops, and all of their equipment. But German military planners could not agree over where all of these troops and equipment would be landing: Would the invasion take place in the Calais area, or on the Normandy beaches? Even though the High Command had evidence that the invasion would take place in Normandy, Adolf Hitler remained convinced that the landings would be somewhere near Calais. At this stage, Hitler was basing his decisions upon intuition instead of evidence.

The interior of Room 5235 of the Justice Department Building, Washington, D.C., during the trial of the eight Operation Pastorius defendants. Attorney General Francis Biddle is examining some documents pertaining to the case. To his right sits FBI Director J. Edgar Hoover, who was present at the prosecution's table nearly every day of the trial. Colonel Carl Ristine, George Dasch's defense counsel, is seated at lower right.

Each of these tiny black rectangles is actually a microphotograph of a document. Microphotography allowed secret memos or reports on classified activities, such as convoy sailings, to be hidden inside a book or a magazine. The innocent-looking package would then be mailed to a contact in Germany. Microphotographs were widely used for sending documents out of the country.

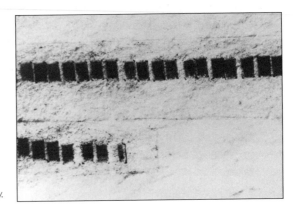

Lieutenant General George S. Patton, Jr., commander of the First U.S. Army Group (FUSAG). FUSAG supposedly consisted of 150,000 men and their equipment, stationed in Kent and Sussex, who were assigned to land in the region of Calais on D-Day. But, in fact, FUSAG was nothing more than an elaborate ruse. It did not exist, except to make the Germans believe that the invasion of France would not take place in Normandy. Although agents in Britain were able to discover that FUSAG was a fake, and reported this information to their superiors in Germany, Hitler and his senior officers paid no attention.

Radio sets like this one, built into a suitcase, were used by agents in the United States, Britain, and South America. They were small, compact, and portable—if an agent had to move suddenly, he could take his radio with him.

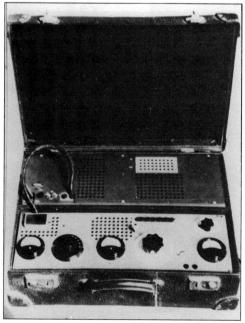

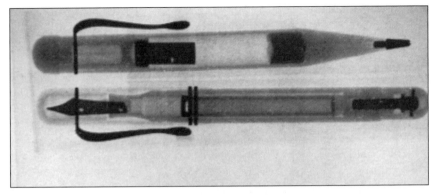

X-rays revealed that an innocent-looking pen-and-pencil set was actually a time fuse.

A clock detonator. This delayed-action device could be wired to an explosive charge and set to trigger the charge several hours, or even several days, afterward.

On the morning of June 13, 1942, Coastguardsman John C. Cullen stumbled across George Dasch and the group from *U-202* while on a routine beach patrol. Dasch deliberately aroused Cullen's suspicions—he had been under orders to kill any such intruder. Cullen reported the incident to his superiors. (And was awarded the Legion of Merit, which he wears in this photo.) This was Dasch's first act in revealing the sabotage plot.

The eight Operation Pastorius defendants went on trial for sabotage, illegal entry into the country, and other lesser charges. Here, Richard Quirin is escorted to room 5235, the setting for the military trial, by two soldiers. Each defendant was moved from his cell to the improvised courtroom in this manner—singly, with two soldiers escorting. The trial was carried out in strict secrecy; no word of the proceedings was released to the public or the press.

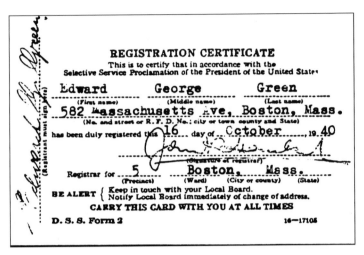

Before being sent abroad, agents were issued a complete set of identification papers: birth certificate, driving license, passport, draft card. Although counterfeit, these documents were usually of such high quality that they appeared to be authentic. Here is a copy of Erich Gimpel's draft card, issued to Edward George Green, Gimpel's cover name.

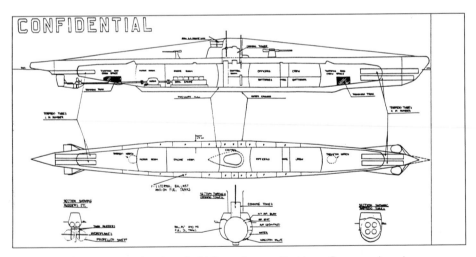

A U.S. government drawing of a U-Boat of unspecified type. German submarines were designed for efficiency, not comfort; every square foot of space was designed for fighting. There was no room for passengers. Agents being transported to North America had to share a bunk with crew members. A 17-day Atlantic crossing, which George Dasch had to endure, was anything but a pleasure cruise.

CHAPTER 3

Double-Cross and Triple-Cross

· · · · ·

THE ABWEHR SENT TRAINED AGENTS TO BRITAIN AS WELL AS TO THE UNITed States. These were in addition to the Irish Republican Army recruits.

Many of these agents were poorly trained and poorly instructed. Some were just unlucky. For whatever reason, almost all of them fell into the hands of either Scotland Yard or British counterintelligence, MI.5.

Petty details were the undoing of some. One would-be spy was picked up when he gave his waitress ration coupons after eating in a London restaurant—the Abwehr did not tell him that coupons were not required in British restaurants. An agent in the United States almost gave himself away when he was asked what kind of bread he wanted with his breakfast; his training course had not mentioned that different kinds of bread were available in the United States.

When German agents were caught, one of two things happened. The unlucky character was either hanged as a spy or—usually—was put to work for MI.5, working against Admiral Canaris and his staff by sending genuine-sounding reports back to Germany that contained false information.

One of the Abwehr's most remarkable agents, or at least most colorful, went by the name of Hans Hansen. He was also known as Hans Schmidt.

Hansen parachuted into England from a specially stripped-down version of a twin-engined Heinkel He 111 bomber. He and another Abwehr employee, a young Swede named Goesta Caroli, landed just outside Salisbury on September 3, 1940. Goesta Caroli was not able to follow through on his assignment, but Hansen kept up communications with Germany until 1945.

Originally, Hansen was sent in advance of "Operation Sea Lion," the anticipated invasion of England. He was assigned to report on enemy resistance and troop movements during the Wehrmacht's advance, and to stay on as a member of the Abwehr's British branch during the occupation—he had an excellent command of the English language, even though he was born in Denmark. Operation Sea Lion never took place, but Hansen kept sending in his reports.

During the next five years, Hansen sent over 1,000 reports. They ranged in subject from the position of barrage balloons and military preparations for the Dieppe raid and the D-Day invasion to the price of bread in Britain. (This last item struck Hansen as being rather trite: "Don't you have anything better to ask?" he signaled the Abwehr.)

His messages also contained other items—personal messages, including the news that he had fathered a seven-pound son; scoldings, especially when promised payments for services rendered were not made on time; and a lot of four-letter words, his favorite being "shit." ("I shit on Germany and its whole fucking Secret Service!" was one outburst.)

In short, Hans Hansen not only got the job done, but he did it with flair. The Abwehr—Hansen usually made contact with the Hamburg branch—was more than satisfied with their man in England and the information he continued to send. He was awarded the Iron Cross First Class for his spy activities in the British Isles.

The Abwehr regarded Hansen as their super spy, capable of getting just about any information asked for: weather reports; observations of military sites, including airfields; and other "extremely valuable" bits of information. His frequent verbal abuse only served to make him more human and appealing.

He was just as well thought of by his enemies. A French writer said that Hansen "evaded the snares of the counterespionage for four years," and also "carried out the policy of integration to the point of marrying an Englishwoman and becoming the father of a British subject."

Another writer credited Hansen with the cleverness of getting a cover job on a farm, where he fell in love with the farmer's daughter and married her. In between his busy domestic and agricultural life, he kept busy with valuable investigations on strategic military matters.

All in all, Hans Schmidt sounds like a miracle man. He did a brilliant job under difficult circumstances, right under the enemy's nose, and still managed to find the time to start a family.

But in the early 1970s, the Hungarian-born American writer Ladislas Farago disclosed that Hansen had actually been working for British counterintelligence, MI.5, throughout the war. According to Mr. Farago, Hansen had been picked up by MI.5 very shortly after coming to earth near Salisbury, and was put to work by "Double-X."

The "Double-Cross" team convinced Hansen to send phony information to Hamburg in his reports. These false messages contained either untrue but genuine-sounding information to mislead the Germans, or else truthful bits of data that would be of little use to them. At any rate, all of the signals sent by Hans Hansen were of almost no value. At least this is how Mr. Farago interpreted events.

But this subterfuge went on for too long to be believed. From September 1940 to May 1945, Hansen sent his reports to Hamburg. These reports were checked and rechecked; no fault was ever found with any of them.

In fact, a special panel was organized to examine Hansen's information. The panel was made up of some very experienced and skeptical intelligence officers and communication specialists. Even a psychiatrist was called in. They went over Hansen's signals for any sign of falseness or irregularities, and couldn't find any. The panel judged Hansen's information to be genuine. After the investigation, the director of the Abwehr's Hamburg section recommended to Admiral Canaris that Hansen be awarded the German Cross in Gold.

But besides the panel's findings, Hansen's sudden defection to the British side raises doubts. Hansen had been a loyal Nazi in his native Denmark, a storm trooper with such strong attachments to his party that he was driven out of the country and fled to Germany. Yet he is supposed to have switched sides after "a long and friendly discussion" with members of British counterintelligence.

Either the boys at MI.5 were *very* persuasive, or Hans Hansen had something up his sleeve.

Counterintelligence also had a long conversation with Hansen's partner, Goesta Caroli, and seemed to have persuaded him to send false information as well. But in December 1940, Caroli tried to escape "Double-X." He made an attempt to break out of the shelter where he was being held under guard, but was caught and put in prison.

Hans Hansen was no less dedicated than Goesta Caroli. He just went about escaping "Double-X" in his own way. Instead of trying to break out of England, which was almost certain to fail, Hansen decided to try his luck at double-crossing "Double-X."

It is very likely that Hans Hansen was actually triple-crossing MI.5—sending genuine messages buried within the phony messages he concocted to satisfy British counterintelligence. Such a scheme would certainly have appealed to Hansen's devious nature and would also explain his "instant transformation" from dedicated German agent to British counterspy. It would also explain why the officers in charge of the Abwehr's Hamburg branch were so well satisfied with Hansen's information for nearly five years.

Such a triple-cross happened in the United States, also involving a German agent. A Dutchman named Walter Koehler, also known as Albert van Loop, came to the United States in the summer of 1942. He had come via Madrid and Portugal, crossing the Atlantic aboard a Portuguese steamer. The Abwehr had sent him. His job was to report on the development of nuclear energy in the United States.

Walter Koehler was another of the Abwehr's "ideal" agents. He was an experienced spy, having done service for the Kaiser in World War I, and had lived in the United States as a "sleeper" agent until June 1941, when he was recalled. In addition, Koehler was Dutch and a Roman Catholic, which provided an excellent cover for him to pass as a refugee.

The Abwehr gave Koehler a quick schooling in nuclear physics, a substantial amount of money, and sent him back to the United States to ferret out atomic secrets.

When he arrived in Madrid, his first step on the way to America, Koehler presented himself, along with his wife, at the American vice consul's office to request visas. But what he actually requested was political asylum.

Koehler described himself to the vice consul as "an employee of the Abwehr," confessing himself to be a German spy. He went on to say that he was being sent to the United States to set up a secret radio transmitter, and that his job would be to send reports of troop movements back to Germany.

To convince the quizzical consul that he was telling the truth, Koehler showed all the Abwehr-issue equipment he had brought along to do his job; his radio operator's manual; a prayer book that served as the basis for the code he was to use in sending messages; chemicals for making invisible ink; a document containing a message written in invisible ink; and other useful tools of the spy trade. The crowning touch was the money supplied by the Abwehr—$6,200.

He had no desire to spy for the Nazis, Koehler said. He only agreed to the assignment so that he could get back to the United States and away from the Nazis—his status as an anti-Nazi Roman Catholic did not offer much hope for a bright future. He told the vice consul that he wanted permission to enter the United States as a refugee.

In return, Koehler said that he would be glad to work for the American cause. He would pretend to work for the Abwehr, going through the motions of doing the assignment he had been sent to perform, while actually sending useless information. This would be his own way of fighting the Nazis.

The American vice consul passed Koehler's request for asylum, as well as his unusual story, along to the State Department in Washington, D.C. When FBI Director J. Edgar Hoover heard about Walter Koehler, he jumped at the chance to get his hands on a cooperative double-agent, especially since it would require no effort on his part. Hoover asked the State Department to grant Koehler's visa.

Koehler entered the United States in an unscheduled and somewhat roundabout way. He left Lisbon in August 1942, on board a Portuguese steamer bound for New York. But during the Atlantic crossing, Koehler became dangerously ill from pneumonia. Because there were no competent medical staff on board, the captain hoisted the international distress signal, hoping that a passing boat would see it and come to assist.

A U.S. Coast Guard received the distress signal off the coast of Florida and went to investigate. When the problem was discovered, the captain of the Coast Guard vessel took Koehler on board and rushed him to a Florida hospital, where he recovered completely.

The Coast Guard may have saved Koehler's life, but only served to make life more difficult for the FBI. When the Portuguese ship docked in New York, the federal agents who met it discovered no

Walter Koehler on board. It took quite a bit of search and worry, and a few well-chosen words by J. Edgar Hoover, before Koehler was located in Florida.

After Koehler recovered from his pneumonia, the FBI set him up as its very own German spy, just as MI.5 did with Hans Hansen. The bureau built Koehler his own radio station on Long Island and surrounded it with a wall of security. The station, in a large house with surrounding grounds, was strictly off-limits to everybody except a few approved federal agents. Guard dogs patrolled the estate. Three federal men ate, slept, and lived at the house, each keeping an eight-hour watch on Koehler and the radio.

Koehler didn't even send out the radio messages to Germany—Hoover didn't trust him. The station was operated by a team of FBI radio technicians and German-language experts. One agent, the one who actually sent the reports, had learned to imitate Koehler's "fist," his touch on the Morse telegraph key.

The first signal was sent by federal agents on February 7, 1943; Koehler was not present. A reply was sent by the Abwehr's Hamburg section five days later. The sender in Hamburg conveyed his "thanks and good wishes," but admonished Koehler to use "caution and discretion" in carrying out future assignments.

Future assignments certainly were carried out with caution and discretion; the FBI saw to that. The federal agents sent a steady stream of reports to Germany. Some of the information was true, military and industrial data that had been cleared by the armed forces as harmless. Most of the remaining reports were misleading and generally useless.

Among the items sent to Hamburg were: weather reports, information about ships under construction and undergoing repair, and troop departures for the British Isles, along with unit insignia. Most of this would either become common knowledge to the Abwehr—U.S. Army insignia for instance, would not remain secret very long after D-Day, and Americans were taken prisoner by the Wehrmacht—or else was doctored to alter the facts, or was a complete fiction.

No information regarding work on the atomic bomb was ever sent. Soviet spies, and Americans sympathetic to the Soviet Union, were able to smuggle atomic secrets to Russia, but there is no record of a single atomic secret ever reaching Germany. The Abwehr, however, seemed happy with the reports it was receiving.

If the Abwehr was happy, the FBI was absolutely ecstatic. The ruse was working perfectly; the Germans were swallowing it whole. Hamburg sent "Koehler" congratulations on a job well done on several occasions, as well as birthday wishes, Christmas greetings, and other pleasantries. The federal agents, nothing if not decent chaps, replied with their own best wishes and fond regards. They could afford to be cordial; they were doing a first-rate job of hoodwinking, misleading, and otherwise making total fools of the Abwehr.

The ruse continued, right through the war. Even after Canaris was removed from his post as Abwehr director in February 1944, "Koehler" kept sending. In the spring of 1944, for instance, he informed Hamburg that "a number of armored and infantry divisions" that were originally slated to be sent to England, as part of the build-up for D-Day, were being diverted instead to the Mediterranean for a "special operation." There was no such operation, of course. It was just one more bit of phony information sent to fool the Germans.

Koehler was not the only spy in the United States. Nine genuine "senior agents" were also at work, along with lesser agents, as well as amateurs connected with the German-American Bund and the Irish Republican Army. But "Koehler" maintained contact with the Abwehr longer than any of the others. He kept sending his reports until the spring of 1945, when the Third Reich finally collapsed.

During all this time, Walter Koehler seemed fairly content to sit by and let the FBI send false information in his name. He and his wife lived in a New York hotel, subsisting fairly comfortably on an allowance which was doled out from the Abwehr funds that had been confiscated by the American authorities.

Some of the federal agents assigned to keep an eye on him did not trust him entirely. He always seemed to have more money than his allotted stipend, although nobody could figure out where it came from, and his behavior seemed a little shadowy and furtive for a simple Dutch refugee. But there was nothing more than vague suspicions, with nothing concrete to go on.

The director of the FBI, J. Edgar Hoover, had no such suspicions. He was quite pleased with himself for having used this "employee of the Abwehr" to suit his own ends. He had Koehler right where he wanted him—at his mercy, "with a pistol in his back," to use his own words.

Hoover was so proud of his work in the Koehler affair that he wrote a magazine article about it—*The Spy Who Double-Crossed Hitler,* which appeared in *American* magazine in May 1946. In the article, Hoover described how he and his bureau had fooled the Abwehr by sending falsified information. He also claimed to have used Koehler to discover how the Abwehr paid its agents in the United States. In addition, he had misled the German High Command over the time and place of the D-Day landings. According to Hoover, he had "succeeded on all scores" with the Koehler hoax.

It was not until many years after the war had ended that an investigator (again Ladislas Farago) made a startling discovery—Koehler hadn't been double-crossing Hitler. He had been triple-crossing J. Edgar Hoover and the Federal Bureau of Investigation.

Koehler's entire "double-agent" ploy, as well as his request for asylum, had been prearranged by the Abwehr. The story he handed to the vice consul in Madrid had been worked out in advance—it would be certain to gain him entry to the United States. And his role as a willing participant in FBI counterespionage had also been rehearsed; it provided the perfect cover for his real assignment.

While federal agents were sending falsified information to Hamburg in Koehler's name, Koehler himself was sending genuine reports to the Abwehr's station in Paris. Hamburg knew all along that the messages it was receiving were phony.

Koehler managed this very effective bit of subterfuge with the help of a contact—just as the man responsible for delivering the plans of the Norden bombsight, Hermann Lang, used a contact to smuggle his drawings out of the United States. Most of Koehler's reports were sent out of the country via couriers, who crossed the Atlantic aboard ships flying a neutral flag. Koehler's couriers would arrive at a port in Spain or Portugal and have his secret information in German-occupied Paris within a few days.

If some piece of information was too important to be sent via steamer-bound courier, Koehler had another method of sending. He had access to a secret radio transmitter in Rochester, New York, which was operated by another Abwehr contact. When Koehler sent for the man from Rochester, he would come to Manhattan to pick up the information and send it off to Paris as soon as he returned to Rochester. To avoid their radio signal being detected, the Rochester station was only used for information that was too vital to be sent by the conventional method.

This went on for over two years, from February 1943 to the end of April 1945. While federal agents were going through an elaborate ritual of ineffectual cloak-and-dagger on Long Island, Walter Koehler was carrying out his own operations right under their noses. And J. Edgar Hoover never caught on.

Federal agents observing Koehler were right when they thought that he had more money than he was supposed to have. For although he had turned $6,000 over to the American authorities, he had neglected to mention that the Abwehr had supplied him with $16,000. Koehler's corpulent wife had smuggled the additional $10,000 in her girdle, right past the federal agents and everybody else. It supplemented the FBI's allowance very nicely and allowed Mr. and Mrs. Koehler to live very comfortably.

Although Koehler never had access to any atomic secrets, his information was a delight to the Abwehr—German Intelligence officers considered him the best spy the Abwehr had during the war.

After Canaris had been removed as Abwehr director, the new head, Walter Schellenberg, decided to revamp the agency. A good many active agents were found to be wanting in the accuracy of their reports and were turned out to pasture. But even Schellenberg, who distrusted on principle any agent who had served under Canaris, considered Walter Koehler one of the Abwehr's best.

"The Spy Who Double-Crossed Hitler" had put one over on the FBI, thoroughly and completely. And this was done during a critical period in the war—during the build-up for D-Day, when U.S. troops and supplies were pouring into England and the German High Command was in dire need of information concerning their movements from the United States. And nobody—not J. Edgar Hoover or MI.5—ever had the slightest suspicion.

Hans Hansen was certainly capable of a similar ploy with British Intelligence.

For one thing, he had access to a great deal of information that would greatly interest the Abwehr. He was also actually *given* access to secret information—this was part of MI.5's method, allowing a double-agent to "play spy." Allowing the agent access was thought to give his phony report to Germany an authentic ring, more genuine-sounding than if MI.5 simply supplied the information.

Hansen was once asked to get some material on factories in a London suburb. MI.5 arranged for him to visit those factories, so that Hansen could get the data first-hand, and in a subversive manner. This is the way a "real" German spy would get his information.

This may have been considered a smart bit of planning by MI.5. It did result in more true-to-life reports, but it also allowed Hansen to see more than counterintelligence wanted him to see.

And Hansen certainly had the opportunity to send unfiltered messages. Although he had an operator supplied by MI.5, Hansen frequently sent all of his messages. So MI.5 just made it easier for Hansen to get around their "Double-X" system.

Although the messages sent by Hansen were monitored by counterintelligence, there was also a way around this. By embedding a "flower" within his phony messages—a genuine bit of information of vital interest to the Abwehr—he would have got his reports through MI.5's screen. Abwehr officers were trained to recognize a "flower" within a fake message. And Hansen certainly had the wit and cleverness to concoct them.

Walter Koehler sent a message via radio a few days after the D-Day landings, a straight report with no need for a flower. It was a report on the success of the landings as reported in the American news media, with a weather report thrown in for good measure. (Koehler did not believe the news reports.) Although it was sent separately from the phony messages, an Abwehr officer said that the report would have been recognized as genuine, a "flower," even if it had been mixed in with the misinformation sent by federal operators.

It seems more than likely that Hans Hansen was masquerading as a double agent as well, just as Walter Koehler had done, and just as effectively. He had the opportunity, had access to vital information, and had the "flower" method for getting his reports through to the Abwehr.

The two men certainly arrived at their "double-agent" destinations by different routes. Walter Koehler had rehearsed his request for political asylum, while Hans Hansen was picked up by MI.5 accidentally. But they both ended up doing the same thing.

It is not very probable that his reports would have fooled the Abwehr's trained intelligence officers for almost five years if they all had been fake, especially since both Hansen and his communiqués were placed under such intense scrutiny by a special committee. The Abwehr never caught on to the fact that Hansen was double-crossing them, because there never was a double-cross. There was a triple-cross. In all probability, Hansen was another first-rate spy, like Walter Koehler, who was furnishing the Abwehr with valuable data while seeming to be fooling them.

CHAPTER 4

An Operation in America

• • • • •

THE FIRST TIME GEORGE DASCH MET THE OTHER MEN ASSIGNED TO OPERation Pastorius was during the early part of 1942. He had just arrived at the Abwehr's elaborately laid out school for saboteurs at Quenzsee, in Brandenburg, not far from Berlin. Along with the other men chosen for the sabotage operation, Dasch was about to begin an intensive course in handling explosives and sabotage methods.

Dasch's time during the month at Quenzsee was largely spent in learning the practical aspects of sabotage. There were exercises in fuse-making, determining the most damaging methods of placing explosive charges, and similar activities. But his main objective was to size up the others in the group, and to learn all he could about them. If he was going to destroy the Pastorius mission—and Dasch was going to do his best to make it fail—his success would depend upon how far he could use them to accomplish his goal.

Originally, the Pastorius team consisted of 12 men, including Dasch. Three of the 12 were removed from the group during the early stages of training, for various reasons. Two were dismissed by Walter Kappe, who decided to oversee all phases of training himself, because of ineptness in both classroom and field activities. One of the men was suffering nervous exhaustion, the effects of 10 months on the Russian front; the other was a drunk. The third man, a boxer nicknamed "Dempsey" after the American champion Jack Dempsey, was called away for a fight against an Italian middleweight.

A fourth man, by the name of Schmidt, eventually dropped out because of his health. He contracted a painful case of gonorrhea and wound up in a naval hospital in France.

The remaining eight men were divided into two groups of four. Dasch himself was to lead one group. The second unit was to be headed by Edward Kerling, who had lived in the United States from 1929 to 1940.

Kerling was the perfect choice. Not only did he have a first-hand knowledge of the United States, and of Americans and their customs, but he was also a dedicated member of the Nazi Party. He was one of the party's "Old Guard"—one of the first 100,000 to join. Even when he was living in the United States, he kept up his membership, arranging for friends and relatives to pay his annual membership fee.

Since Kerling would not be in the same group, Dasch would not have to worry about him after landing in the United States. But because of Kerling's party loyalty, he would have to be watched very carefully until the training course ended. If Dasch should happen to say or do anything to give himself away, Kerling would not hesitate to hand him over to the Gestapo.

The other three men in Kerling's group were Werner Thiel, Herbert Haupt, and Hermann Neubauer. All of them had lived in the United States at some point in their lives. Haupt had lived there almost 18 years, since he was five years old. Most of the men had worked at mainly menial jobs, although Werner Thiel had been a mechanic. None of them struck Dasch as being exceptionally intelligent. As long as he watched himself, they shouldn't pose much of a threat.

The three in his own group were Ernest Peter Burger, Heinrich Heinck, and Richard Quirin. Heinck and Quirin had each spent 12 years in the United States. Quirin had been a house painter and had worked as a mechanic; while a resident, he had become a naturalized American citizen. Heinck had entered the country without informing the U.S. immigration authorities and had lived and worked as an illegal alien in the German section of New York City.

Ernest Burger struck Dasch as a unique character, and he didn't know exactly what to make of him. Dasch knew that Burger had been a storm trooper, one of the Nazi Party elite, but he also found out that he had spent time in a concentration camp. It wasn't very often that anyone heard of a storm trooper who spent time in a camp. Dasch decided to find out more about Herr Burger.

He saw all seven of the men every day during the training program at Quenzsee. Even though he was under a terrific strain,

Dasch found himself enjoying the course and its various exercises. He found it difficult to pay attention to some of the lectures, however. It wasn't that they were boring; it was just that he realized that the subject matter of the lessons—fuse-making and related topics—would never be put to use.

The sabotage school itself has been compared to a country club—a picturesque 12-room stone house on a lakeside estate, surrounded by lawns and gardens. It was also completely cut off from the outside world, which gave it two advantages. The walled-in estate allowed the trainees to concentrate on their course without any distractions, and it kept prying eyes from seeing what they weren't meant to see.

The country club atmosphere also provided the perfect disguise. No one would have guessed that within the stone walls surrounding the Quenzsee estate were a rifle and pistol range, as well as a grenade-throwing pitch. The estate's lake was used for exercises in boat handling. Bridges, railway tracks, and other likely targets had been built on the grounds, so the trainees could practice their newly learned skills in demolition and sabotage.

Throughout the entire training course, only American English was spoken. American folk songs were sung after hours. American newspapers and magazines were required reading for all the Operation Pastorius candidates, to familiarize the men with current events in the United States. Copies of *Life* magazine and other popular publications arrived regularly at Quenzsee, along with copies of *The New York Times*, *Chicago Tribune*, and several other papers—compliments of the Abwehr's friends in America.

Pistol shooting had originally been included in the Pastorius training program, until Dasch argued that it was a waste of time—to the resentment of Kappe and other Abwehr officers. More practical lessons were given in the making of homemade bombs and incendiary devices. Some of the incendiaries could be made from materials available in any pharmacy—saltpeter and sawdust was one effective combination. They were taught four others, as well.

Other simple explosives and incendiaries were also demonstrated, including powdered sugar mixed with calcium chlorate. After watching demonstrations on how to make these bombs, the men would make their own in the school's laboratory. All of the formulas and mixtures proved to be every bit as effective as the instructors said they would be.

Dasch couldn't work up much enthusiasm for these classes, either. They would be taking their own explosives with them—blocks of plastic-like stuff, which could only be exploded by a special detonator. And anyway, nobody would be making use of any kind of explosives—he would see to that.

In between lectures and demonstrations, Dasch was able to find out something about the mysterious Ernest Peter Burger. It turned out that Burger had run afoul of the secret state police, the Gestapo, who clapped him in "detention" while he was awaiting trial for falsifying documents. The trial never took place, since the charges were completely trumped up, but Burger was left in one of the Gestapo's camps for 17 months.

Burger, understandably, held a grudge against the Nazi regime for his treatment at its hands. He had been a loyal party member since its earliest days, long before the Nazis ever came to power. He had even taken part in the Munich Beer Hall Putsch in 1923, which marked the beginning of Adolf Hitler's rise. The charge that he had falsified documents was an insult; he could have proved his innocence, if anyone had bothered to listen to his side of the story.

The whole thing had been trumped up by the Gestapo, in retaliation for writing a few unkind-but-true reports about Gestapo activities with the population of Poland and Czechoslovakia. He never falsified anything, he insisted. And he had been required to write the reports that caused him all the trouble.

But the crowning indignation was to have been left in a Gestapo camp for nearly a year and a half. Someone in the party should have stepped in on his behalf. No one wanted to get involved, especially since it would have meant arguing with the Gestapo. Apparently, he went on, his loyalty to the party meant nothing.

Dasch was surprised to hear Burger's story. He was also surprised to hear that anyone with his attitude would have been allowed to join Operation Pastorius. It was certainly a lucky break for Dasch—maybe he would be able to use Burger's grudge against the Nazis to further his own ends. After listening to Burger's revelation, with some astonishment, Dasch decided to pay more attention to him than he had before.

After their sabotage course at Quenzsee had been completed, the men were given a 10-day furlough before the next phase of their training began. Dasch went home to visit his relatives. He told his mother that he would not be able to visit her for a while, and probably wouldn't be able to write, either. He did not want to tell her the reason why, though. Instead, he said that he was being transferred to a government post in Chile, which he hoped would put her mind at ease.

In the middle of May 1942, Dasch and the other eight men were summoned by Walter Kappe again. This time, they were to report to him in Berlin. Kappe had arranged to take his eight saboteurs on several field trips throughout Germany, which would provide the finishing touch for their intensified training course. Kappe decided to go along with the men, mainly to impress his superiors with his leadership qualities.

The first of these trips was to the I. G. Farben aluminum plant in Bitterfield. They also visited the plant in Aachen. Both plants were practically replicas of the Aluminum Company of America's plants in the United States, which the Pastorius team were being sent to destroy. In fact, the same engineers and technicians who had supervised the construction of the American plants were on hand to conduct the tours. They also had photos and plans of the factories and their power systems. These were used to brief the men in the most effective ways of destroying the plants.

Knocking out the aluminum factories was a fairly straightforward job, the Pastorius team was told. The best way would be to cut off the power supply. If the electricity were stopped for eight to ten hours, all the aluminum in the electrolytic baths, in which the metal was refined, would solidify. The result would be one solid, useless block of aluminum.

After the metal had solidified, the only way to remove it was to use dynamite, which would also destroy the baths. Farben's engineers estimated that it would take from eight to ten months for the factories to recover. No aluminum could be produced for the American aircraft industry until the damage had been repaired.

To cut off the power supply, the simplest method would be to blow up one of the high-tension towers that supplied the factories with electricity. Technicians advised the Pastorius men to pick a tower out in rough, open country, miles away from everything. Not only would it be left unguarded, but it would also be difficult for crews to reach and repair—at least eight hours to find and put back in working condition.

After the Farben tours, which lasted four days, the men were taken to another lecture/demonstration. This one was at Berlin's railway repair center, where they were given a thorough briefing on the rail network in the eastern United States. But the main point was to describe the rail system's most vulnerable points, and how to knock out switches, tracks, and signals at these points.

The instructors were the chief engineer of the Berlin rail yard, as well as a man named Reinhold Barth, who had been an employee of New York's Long Island Railroad for nine years. Barth, who was truly an expert on American trains and rail systems, was also George Dasch's cousin by marriage.

Sabotaging locomotives was another subject. The methods ranged from the simple, such as throwing sand into the engine's bearings, to the complex: using dynamite to blow up the engine. A favorite technique involved the yellow plastic explosives that the eight men would be taking with them. If a chunk of this were painted black, it would look like a small lump of coal. It would then be thrown into a coal tender, where it would eventually explode inside a locomotive's firebox.

By this time, the Pastorius team was only a week away from its departure for the United States. There were no more lectures or demonstrations to attend, but there were a million small details to be dealt with. And Dasch still hadn't decided what to do about wrecking the operation.

One item to be taken care of was the cover stories that the men would use after landing in the United States. The stories had to be kept fairly uncomplicated; the men only had a week to get used to them.

Dasch became George John Day, born in San Francisco in 1900. Edward Kerling became Edward J. Kelly, also born in San Francisco before the 1906 earthquake. Kappe wanted the false birthdates to be pre-earthquake in case proof were ever demanded by U.S. officials—the men could claim that the records had been destroyed in the devastating quake and resulting fire.

Each man's fictitious story included the actual details of the time spent in the United States. The years spent in Germany were changed, however, to make it seem that the men had lived their entire lives in the United States. Cover names were kept close to each man's real name; Quirin became Richard Quintas, born in Lisbon.

False identification documents were also issued. Ernest Burger kept his real identity, since he was a naturalized American citizen, but his passport was altered to make it look as though he had never left the United States.

Herbert Haupt, also a naturalized American, kept his identity, as well. But he did not have a draft card, which would have been a serious offense in wartime, so he was given a forged card. After he returned to Chicago, he would register with his local draft board and be issued a genuine card.

Issuing the eight men with American clothes, made in the United States and with actual American labels, presented no problems—the Abwehr had its own clothing warehouse, filled with everything from overcoats to underwear. When the men landed on the American coast, however, they would be wearing navy work uniforms—if they were picked up on the beach, they would be held in internment camps as prisoners of war. In civilian clothes, they would be treated as spies and subject to execution.

There was also the matter of money to finance the operation. Dasch would carry $30,000 in cash, sewn into the lining of his suitcase. Edward Kerling, in charge of the second group, carried $70,000. Each man carried $5,000 hidden in money belts—100 fifty dollar bills.

While the men were being prepared for the landing in America, the Abwehr's laboratory had its own job to do. The yellow plastic explosive bricks were sealed in waterproof cases, to protect them while buried at the water's edge. A variety of detonators had also been made ready. These consisted of several types of fuses and timers, including a clock that could delay an explosion for as long as 14 days. Each of the sabotage teams was to get three cases of plastic explosives and one case of fuses and timers.

There was a final briefing in Berlin for George Dasch and Edward Kerling, which covered a few small but important details. At the briefing, the two were given the address of their contact in Lisbon, as well as several useful people who lived in the United States. One of these was a "supposed clergyman" who lived in Hoboken, New Jersey. Everything was written in invisible ink on silk handkerchiefs; the writing would appear if the handkerchief were held over heat, such as a radiator.

All eight men were given a farewell dinner by their Abwehr superiors. It was a fairly lavish affair, held in Berlin's Tiergarten restaurant and attended by Col. von Lahousen. Walter Kappe, never one to turn down a free drink, was also there. The food at the dinner was first rate, and there were many toasts and speeches, but Dasch didn't enjoy it very much. He had too much to worry about.

A farewell that meant a great deal more to Dasch was from his fellows in the anti-Nazi resistance movement, whom he had first met while working in the Seehaus. They all wished him the best of luck in his attempt to foil the sabotage operation, although some warned him that he might be biting off a bit more than he could chew.

Dasch had thought of this himself. In fact, he had thought of little else for the past several weeks. He knew that he had seven men against him and that he had better be damn careful not to tip his hand.

One of his Seehaus chums also warned him that he was leaving himself wide-open to the "glory-grabbers" if he planned on reporting Operation Pastorius to the American law enforcement authorities. Some big noise might try to take all the credit for "capturing" the saboteurs, at Dasch's expense. But he just laughed off the warning.

"You don't know America the way I do," he replied. "Everything is going to be all right." It was a conversation that he would remember.

Dasch and the rest of the Pastorius team left for France on May 22—Walter Kappe also came along, in his role as Pastorius leader. On their way to the submarine base at Lorient, which would be their port of departure for the United States, the men stopped in Paris for the weekend. Kappe told everybody to "go out and have a good time." They certainly obeyed this order, with a vengeance. It was in Paris that Josef Schmidt, one of the men originally in Dasch's group, came down with gonorrhea, and had to be sent to a naval hospital for treatment.

Following their Paris blow-out, the eight men of Operation Pastorius, along with Walter Kappe, staggered into Lorient. There, the two teams split up. Edward Kerling's group was to land on the coast of Florida, and would cross the Atlantic aboard

U-584. Dasch's group was to make the crossing on *U-202*. But the submarine was still in dry-dock, which meant that everybody would have to stay in Lorient a little longer than planned. The waiting got on everyone's nerves.

Their nerves were not helped by the discovery that some of the U.S. currency they were carrying was worthless. The non-negotiable bills were $50 gold certificates, which had been withdrawn from circulation in 1933, when the United States went off the gold standard. It turned out that most of the money was perfectly acceptable, and that the gold certificates had slipped in by accident. But the incident didn't help to bolster anyone's confidence.

George Dasch went through a nerve-wrenching experience of his own. When he arrived in Lorient, he discovered that he had left his wallet and tobacco pouch on the train from Paris. Inside were items that could cause all sorts of trouble if they fell into the wrong hands. The pouch contained a photo of the Pastorius trainees, taken at Quenzsee, which he planned to give to the American authorities. The wallet held his forged U.S. draft card.

The discovery rattled Dasch, who was of a naturally nervous disposition to begin with. As soon as he discovered his loss, he rushed off to the railway station, and reported the missing items to the railway police.

Dasch's statement was rambling and incoherent. Instead of being helpful, the police were suspicious of Dasch and his stammering explanation. The sergeant demanded to see his identity papers. Because he would be leaving the country within a few days, Dasch didn't have any. The sergeant's suspicions turned to alarm. He called the captain, who called the Gestapo. At Dasch's insistence, he also telephoned Walter Kappe.

Kappe came down to the station, and managed to talk Dasch out of his jam. After everything had been cleared up and Dasch was allowed to leave, Kappe regaled him with an outraged speech about his carelessness and stupidity. Dasch was shaken and angered by the incident, but it was a lot better than being inside a Gestapo prison. He never did get his wallet and tobacco pouch back.

By this time, Edward Kerling and his three men were on their way to Brest, where they would board *U-584*. Dasch and his group— Ernest Burger, Richard Quirin, and Heinrich Heinck—squeezed through the hatchway of *U-202* on May 26.

To shield the U-Boat from prying eyes on the shore, a freighter had been anchored between the dock and the submarine. The four men, dressed in navy work clothes, had to board the freighter before they could cross over and climb onto *U-202*. If anyone happened to see Dasch and the other three men clambering up the merchant-man's gangplank, no one would have suspected who the men were or what they were doing.

Walter Kappe had also come out to Lorient. He drove himself to the port from Paris, to deliver a few last words—as though the men hadn't heard enough of them in the past few weeks. After his little speech, Kappe got back in his car and drove off, and the *U-202* made ready for sea.

Lieutenant Commander Lindner, *U-202's* commanding officer, had no idea what his destination was. His sealed orders had been delivered at dockside by an Abwehr officer, along with instructions not to open them until he was well out to sea. When he finally opened his orders, the instructions specified that he was to run his subma-rine to the northeastern coast of the United States, to Southampton, New York, on Long Island.

When *U-202* was off the Long Island coast, Lindner was to take the boat as close to shore as possible. His four passengers would then be put ashore in a rubber boat. Because he would have to bring the submarine so close to land, and on the surface, a night landing would be necessary.

The orders also prohibited Lindner from giving his crew any details of Operation Pastorius. He only told the men that the four strangers on board were to be shown every courtesy, but added that they were not to be questioned. When *U-202* returned to Lorient, Lindner continued, no mention was to be made of the men's presence on board. To emphasize the secrecy of the operation that was just beginning, Lindner warned that anyone who disregarded this order would be punished by death.

At first, George Dasch thought that Lindner was "a very Nazi type, with an Iron Cross dangling at his neck." But during the crossing, the two seemed to get along together very well. As *U-202* cruised out of Lori-ent, Lindner allowed Dasch to come up to the conning tower and watch as the boat headed for the open sea. Dasch took mental notes of the dock facilities, the harbor defenses, and especially the submarine pens, which he knew would be useful to the American anti-U-Boat campaign.

While his submarine was within range of land-based aircraft from England, Lindner ran submerged during the day. At night, however, he came to the surface, to recharge the batteries and ventilate the boat. But as soon as the U-Boat reached mid-Atlantic, *U-202* ran on the surface day and night. The only time the boat ran submerged was during the twice-daily crash-dive practice alarm, which sent the crew scrambling for their battle stations and the boat plunging toward the ocean floor.

At this stage of the Battle of the Atlantic, the U-Boats controlled the sea lanes, especially the area in mid-ocean, which was out of range of enemy planes. There was little fear of Allied anti-submarine methods. The best precaution against British or American destroyers was a sharp-eyed lookout.

During the crossing, Burger, Quirin, and Heinck were cooped up in the crew's quarters. They had to share bunks with the U-Boat's men and could only sleep while the bed's full-time occupant was on duty. Every square foot of the submarine's space was accounted for; there was no room on board for three additional bunks.

Dasch lived in the officers' quarters, which were a lot more comfortable. He had hoped to have a few words with Ernest Burger while on board, to sound him out on his anti-Nazi feelings and, just possibly, to confide in him about what to do about Operation Pastorius. But because he was separated from the other two, he would not be able to talk to Burger. The only place where he could have a conversation would have been in the crowded crew's quarters, which was hardly practical with what he had to say.

For the first few days after leaving Lorient, Dasch was too seasick to do any talking, anyway. So were the other Pastorius men. Even using the toilet turned out to be a chore. Getting into the sub's "head" involved crawling through a very small hatchway, and then twisting and bending until the objective had been reached. Flushing the toilet required turning several valves and pulling levers, all of which had to be done in proper sequence. Anyone who did it right the first time was awarded a small diploma of achievement.

Dasch and his three-man crew spent 17 days aboard *U-202*; it seemed like a lot longer. At least Dasch could go up to the conning tower for some fresh air once in a while. He was also allowed into the radio compartment, so that he could tune into news broadcasts from the United States—he said it was to prepare him for American life, although he kept his eyes open for any classified documents that might be out. But Burger, Quirin, and Heinck were left to their own devices, which consisted mainly of trying to sleep between bouts of seasickness.

As *U-202* plowed its way toward North America, Dasch went over the landing procedure with the other three men. One of the main concerns was placing all the cases, especially the boxes containing the explosives, aboard the rubber raft without capsizing it. Once they got on the beach, they would bury the explosives. Later, Dasch told them, they would come back and dig them up, after they had made contact with their friends in the United States and arranged for transportation.

At this point, they were only a few days away from their destination. The nearness of the event gave all four a new case of the jitters. Dasch, however, was feeling a different sort of nervousness than the other three.

Off the coast of Nova Scotia, *U-202* ran into some fairly dense fog, which forced Lindner to reduce speed. He had hoped to land his four guests on Thursday, June 11, but the fog would delay that event.

A further delay occurred when Lindner decided—against orders—to give chase to a freighter that was reported in the area. he reluctantly gave up when it became obvious that he would never find his quarry in the fog.

On June 12, *U-202* reached its destination. Lindner gave the order, and the boat submerged. For the next five hours, the submarine would lie in 100 feet of water, on the bottom of the Atlantic ocean off the coast of Long Island.

George Dasch was all too aware that he would be going ashore in a few hours. He had given a lot of thought about what to do to derail Operation Pastorius, and he had a vague idea of getting in touch with the Federal Bureau of Investigation. But before he did anything, he wanted to find out how Ernest Burger felt about his plan. It would be reassuring to have an ally, which would also mean one less man against him.

Even if Burger did agree to go along with him, he would still have to be extremely careful not to reveal himself to Quirin and Heinck. Dasch knew that he was in a tight spot, but he did not fully realize how tight a spot he was really in.

CHAPTER 5

An Agent Sitting in the War Cabinet

· · · · ·

JUST AS THE FEDERAL BUREAU OF INVESTIGATION TIRELESSLY CLAIMED that no enemy agent ever had any success inside the United States, and that every factory fire and explosion "of suspicious origin" was the result of an accident or carelessness, British counterintelligence would insist that no German secret agent remained at large in Britain. According to MI.5, every German agent that landed, either by submarine or parachute, was picked up by security forces within days, before the agent could possibly send any messages back to Germany.

Nobody likes to admit failure. Intelligence agencies seem especially reluctant to talk about their less-than-successful efforts, and MI.5 is no exception.

Despite the claim that not a single enemy agent escaped detection, several Abwehr "employees" did elude MI.5, and inflicted no small amount of damage to the British war effort. Counterintelligence leaders were well aware of this, but they continued to deny that any Abwehr agents outsmarted them. Sometimes they deliberately lied to cover up the truth; sometimes they simply ignored the fact that German agents were at work in Britain—officially, at least.

During the early part of the war, a frequent Abwehr ploy was to send agents disguised as refugees. One such agent was Jan Willen Ter Braak, or Jan Willem Ter Brank, who came to Britain claiming to be a refugee from the Netherlands.

According to the official MI.5 story, Ter Brank arrived in the guise of a Dutch botanist. He duly registered with the police, providing a Dutch passport and giving a cover story that he had come to do research on the medicinal properties of certain plants. In order to accomplish his research, he explained, he needed access to material on file at Cambridge University. Ter Brank's story was so original that it was accepted at face value, and he was granted permission to stay in England. All this happened in October 1940, when the Luftwaffe was attacking London every night.

Ter Brank was no ordinary spy, according to MI.5. He wasn't any sort of spy, for that matter. He had come to England to carry out a very specific assignment—to assassinate Winston Churchill.

But shortly before Ter Brank showed up in Cambridge, the story goes, a farmer discovered a parachute that had been buried in one of his fields. He reported his find to the police; Scotland Yard investigated all newly arrived foreigners, including the Dutch botanist.

The investigators who watched Ter Brank found that he did spend a good deal of his time doing research at Cambridge University. But he also spent a lot of time in London, especially in the vicinity of the Cabinet War Rooms in Storey's Gate, Westminster, where Churchill and his cabinet had their underground headquarters. The Dutchman also seemed to be on hand whenever Churchill made a public appearance.

The final tip-off came when Ter Brank was sent an incorrectly addressed letter—it was sent to 7 Oxford Street, a nonexistent address, instead of 7 Oxford Road. A search of the Dutchman's lodgings in Oxford Road disclosed a radio transmitter, several code books, two pistols, and other incriminating evidence. Also found were documents which revealed that Ter Brank had been sent with orders to kill Churchill.

Somehow, Ter Brank learned that he had been found out. Rather than face the hangman, he shot himself in the head—"with one of the bullets intended for Churchill." His suicide came very shortly after he had landed by parachute.

And so counterintelligence, ably assisted by Scotland Yard, was able to stop the man who had been sent by Hitler to assassinate Winston Churchill. It is a very dramatic story, featuring a hired Nazi killer, and a heroic Scotland Yard and MI.5, who saved the leader that would see the nation through its wartime crisis.

Official versions usually end like that. But the unofficial story, which did not come to light until decades after the war had ended, is far different.

According to this version, the Dutch agent managed to evade capture for quite a while, probably for over a year. Nobody really knows how long he remained at large in Britain. He did enter Britain as a refugee and went under the name Willen Ter Braak, but MI.5 was never able to determine when or where.

Ter Brank's assignment was not anything as dramatic as the assassination of Winston Churchill. He was sent to observe air bases for the Royal Air Force, which is exactly what he did. He traveled throughout the country, visiting important airfields and keeping his eyes open. After returning to his lodgings in Cambridge, he reported his observations to Germany via his radio transmitter. The RAF was of special interest to the Abwehr during this period, just as Allied shipping would be a short time later.

But besides being an excellent spy, Ter Brank was also apparently mentally unstable. He did commit suicide, just as the official version says, but his motive has never been determined. His body was found in an air raid shelter on April 1, 1941, six weeks before the Luftwaffe's bombing offensive against Britain would end. He had shot himself in the head. Apparently, he had become depressed because he had run out of rationing coupons and money, but nobody knows the real reason.

The police didn't begin to investigate Ter Brank until after his body was discovered. They found his identity papers in his pocket, which gave his address as 7 Oxford Road, and went around to see what they could find. One of the things they found was his radio transmitter. The police contacted Scotland Yard, who got in touch with MI.5, and an in-depth inquiry began.

Counterintelligence discovered that Ter Brank's registration card had been forged, along with his other papers. They were able to confirm that he was not working for "Double-X," and that he was a genuine German agent.

From the bus tickets that were discovered in his personal belongings, MI.5 was able to piece together Ter Brank's movements. He had traveled to the vicinity of a number of the RAF's air bases in England. If the "official" date of Ter Brank's arrival is anything to go by, he was at large from October 1940 to April 1941. This takes up most of the period when the Luftwaffe was conducting its night bombing raids against London and other cities. (The London blitz lasted from September 1940 until May 1941.) But Ter

Brank could have been in the country long before October 1940, and could possibly have sent back reports on RAF activities during the Battle of Britain.

Which means that Ter Brank was sending information about the RAF's airfields, and presumably aircraft and operations, during the time when the German air fleets were especially concerned with British fighter units.

Apart from the fact that Ter Brank traveled to RAF airfields and kept in touch with Germany via radio, nothing else was known about him. The coroner was able to conclude that he was about 27 years old, which was given in his papers. But nobody had any idea of how he had entered Britain, the value of the reports he had sent back to Germany, or even if Jan Willen Ter Braak was his real name.

The "official" version of the story doesn't have very much in common with the facts. It disagrees on nearly every detail: the Dutchman's name (Ter Braak or Brank?); when he landed and where; his cover story (the unofficial version doesn't mention one); motive for suicide; and, most important, his objective and how successful he was in attaining it.

MI.5's version serves two purposes: It makes counterintelligence look heroic, and it covers up the truth. The official version is more dramatic, as well—a story about a hired killer sent to eliminate Churchill is a lot more exciting than a story about somebody sent to watch a bunch of airplanes. But its main aim is to maintain MI.5's "perfect" image, which maintains that counterintelligence caught every Abwehr agent in Britain.

At least two other Abwehr employees claim to have been successful in the espionage business, as well. According to their stories, they parachuted into England, carried out their assignments, and returned to Germany without arousing the suspicions of either MI.5 or Scotland Yard. Although their stories sound plausible, there is no way of checking them either for truth or accuracy.

Enthusiastic amateur spies were sometimes able to outmaneuver MI.5 as effectively as Abwehr-trained professionals. One such agent was an Iraqi army officer named Captain Mahomet Salman. Salman had the perfect cover—he was studying tanks and armored warfare at Sandhurst, Woolwich, and Aldershot, with the full cooperation of the British Army.

Before leaving Iraq in 1938, Salman volunteered his services to the Abwehr. His offer was readily accepted. Not only would Salman have access to highly classified technical information—he was attached to the highly secret Mechanized Warfare Experimental Establishment—he would also be able to send it along to Berlin with no trouble at all.

Salman's routine was to send his reports to Baghdad in the Iraqi diplomatic pouch. They were disguised as letters, and addressed to his brother, Major General Ahmed Salman. The major general, who was the commander of the Iraqi Air Force, passed the letters along to the Abwehr's representative in Baghdad. The Abwehr man radioed the information to Berlin.

Both Capt. Salman and his brother were anti-British and strongly sympathetic to the Nazi regime. Many Arabs resented the presence of British forces in the Middle East. Salman took his resentment out by giving aid and assistance to Britain's enemies.

From March 1938 until May 1941, Salman kept the German High Command well informed of developments in British armored strategy. Salman returned to Iraq in 1941, but rendered invaluable assistance to the Wehrmacht's panzer divisions during his stay in England.

Thanks to Salman, planners in the German army knew all about British armored units and their equipment. And panzer officers knew what to expect when they met British tanks in the field. Salman's information was of assistance to the Wehrmacht during its blitzkrieg through the Low Countries and France in the spring of 1940. Field Marshal Erwin Rommel and his Afrika Korps also benefited from Salman's classified reports during their tank battles with the British in the Libyan desert. And MI.5 never knew a thing about Salman's extra-curricular activities.

Not every spy in England was working for Germany. The Communist Party of Great Britain were just as busy as the Abwehr's agents, but the Communists sent their information to the Soviet Union. The Soviets had a great many supporters in Britain, eager to do anything to help Mother Russia. "The Soviets managed to penetrate virtually every corner of Britain's secret organizations, including MI.5," wrote a specialist on intelligence matters.

One Soviet informer was Douglas Springhall, who sent a great deal of "highly secret" information to Russia. He accomplished this feat right under the noses of MI.5, in spite of the fact that counter-intelligence was keeping him under surveillance because of his politics and suspect national allegiance.

Springhall had been a member of the Communist Party since the 1920s. He had been dismissed from the Royal Navy for spreading dissension among the men. For some time, he had been suspected of passing classified documents to the Soviets, although there was no proof. Actually, MI.5's suspicions were well founded; Springhall was busily engaged in sending information on the workings of the British Secret Service, as well as data on jet engine research.

The man from whom Springhall received his information was Captain Ormond Uren. Capt. Uren's military record would seem to place him above suspicion at first glance. He had even been a British agent himself and parachuted into Hungary earlier in the war. But his political leanings proved stronger than his national loyalty; through Springhall, Capt. Uren supplied the Soviets with as many secrets as he could safely get away with.

MI.5 finally got wise to that arrangement, after months of surveillance, and arrested both men. Springhall was tried in a secret session and in June 1943 was sentenced to seven years in prison for espionage. Capt. Uren was court-martialed for the same offense.

When news of the trial and sentence of Springhall was made public, the reaction from Moscow was outrage. The Soviet ambassador in London lodged a strong protest. Reprisals against the staff at the British Embassy in Moscow were feared, but nothing came of them. Although the Russians were quick to protest the arrest of two of their spies, they did not put an end to their spying, even after the war ended.

One of MI.5's more embarrassing, and costly, failures involved an American named Tyler Kent. Kent worked as a code and cipher clerk at the U.S. Embassy in London's Grosvenor Square.

He had been in the U.S. Diplomatic Corps since the age of 23. He was able to enter the foreign service at that young age because of family connections. His father was also a diplomat and knew many important people in the State Department. Young Kent never had to exert himself to get what he wanted. After attending the best schools and universities, he went straight into a good job in the diplomatic service in 1934.

Two years later, Kent was appointed to a much sought-after post: code and cipher clerk at the American Embassy in Moscow. While he was in Russia, he was able to observe the Communist system from first-hand experience, and he developed a distaste for it that turned into hatred. During the three years he spent in Moscow, Kent began drifting into right-wing politics.

Kent's next appointment came just after the war began, in October 1939. He was transferred to another choice job—cipher clerk at the American Embassy in London. He was responsible for coding and decoding diplomatic correspondence from the State Department in Washington as well as the British Foreign Office.

Shortly after arriving in London, he met a Russian woman named Anna Wolkoff. Kent never had any romantic attachment to Anna Wolkoff, who was nine years his senior and has been described as "perhaps the ugliest and wittiest woman in London." But they did share a right-wing political view—Wolkoff hated Jews and Communists for making her flee Russia for her life—and she introduced Kent to some of her outspoken pro-Fascist friends.

Kent was presented to members of the Right Club, which had been founded by the very right-wing Captain A. H. M. Ramsay. The Right Club believed that Adolf Hitler was the only person who could prevent a Communist-dominated Europe. They also thought that Winston Churchill, who was First Lord of the Admiralty at that time and not yet prime minister, was working hand-in-hand with the Jews and Communists, and that President Franklin D. Roosevelt was helping Churchill to extend the war. The Jew Roosevelt, or "Rosenfelt," wanted to make bigger profits for the Jewish banking interests. Kent heard and believed.

While he was still on the staff of the Moscow embassy, Kent had started a curious pastime—copying and photographing secret documents. When he was transferred to London he destroyed his secret communiqué collection; he didn't want to risk getting caught smuggling them out of Russia. In London, he started on a new batch of documents.

At about the same time that Kent came to London, Franklin D. Roosevelt and Winston Churchill began to correspond with each other, via the State Department's "Gray Code." Kent saw every one of these messages, including the ones from Churchill that were hand-delivered to the American ambassador Joseph P. Kennedy. He also made copies of them. Among the messages was the destroyers-for-bases deal between Churchill and Roosevelt, which sent 50 U.S. Navy destroyers to Britain in exchange for 99-year leases on British bases in Bermuda and other locations.

Actually, at first, Kent didn't realize the importance of some of these messages. In his messages to President Roosevelt, Churchill signed himself "Naval Person." Kent thought the Naval person was some official connected with the Admiralty. Capt. Ramsay informed him who the Naval person really was.

Kent didn't like the tone of the messages, especially after he found out that Churchill was sending them. They usually consisted of requests for aid and assistance from the United States and were filled with gloomy reports on the dire condition of Britain's defenses and armed forces.

Roosevelt's replies didn't do much to reassure Kent, either. He thought that the president was far too sympathetic toward Churchill. Along with many other Americans, he believed that the war was strictly a European affair and that the U.S. should stay out of it. Kent resented Churchill's repeated calls for assistance and liked Roosevelt's responses even less.

Kent began distrusting Roosevelt's foreign policy while he was still in Moscow. He thought the president's policy was "contrary to the interests of the United States."

From what Kent could see, it looked as though the president were trying to drag the United States into the war on his own initiative. His messages to Churchill were kept secret from the State Department and Congress, not to mention the American public.

Roosevelt had promised the country that he would never allow the United States to enter the war, and now he was secretly breaking that promise. Kent thought that the American news media should be filled in on Roosevelt and his clandestine dealings with the Naval Person.

When Kent told Anna Wolkoff about the telegrams, she was highly intrigued. When he said that he had copies of them all, she became positively transfixed and wanted to see them for herself. Kent obliged. She read all of the copies and took many of them away from Kent's flat—she wanted to show them to Capt. Ramsay, she said.

The papers taken by Anna Wolkoff were not limited to the Roosevelt/Churchill papers, although these were of prime interest. Some of the other documents included reports on the strength and disposition of British forces in France, figures on British food and gasoline stocks, future military strategy, and statistics on American aid. "It was almost as if the Germans had an agent sitting in the War Cabinet," according to one authority on espionage.

Anna Wolkoff handed the documents over to a contact in the Italian Embassy. From London, the papers traveled in the diplomatic pouch to the German Embassy in Rome. The German minister, Hans Mackenson, passed them along to Berlin.

British counterintelligence had cracked the German foreign ministry's diplomatic code and was able to decipher Mackenson's reports to Berlin. They knew that the Germans were getting hold of some very sensitive information. But MI.5 had no idea where Mackenson was getting his supply of highly accurate data.

Everything was obviously coming from inside the American Embassy, but nobody knew who the leak was. The police had their eye on Anna Wolkoff because of her right-wing politics—and because of her habit of pasting sticky labels saying "This Is A Jew's War" on bus stops and other public places—but had no reason to link her with the security leak, or with Tyler Kent.

Miss Wolkoff had also been writing to William Joyce, "Lord Haw Haw," the renegade Englishman who made Nazi propaganda broadcasts to Britain. She wrote to him at regular intervals, to praise his broadcasts and to offer suggestions for future broadcasts. This gave Scotland Yard more reason to be interested in her activities, but it still did nothing to connect her with Tyler Kent.

Eventually, after several months of sending copies of classified documents to Germany, Kent and Anna Wolkoff became careless. They began taking Kent's photos of the documents to a photography shop for processing—Kent had been doing the job himself up to that point. Scotland Yard trailed Miss Wolkoff, in the company of the young American, to the shop. After the two left, the detectives went into the shop and found photos and negatives of secret papers.

Another version says Scotland Yard discovered that Kent belonged to the Right Club, which first tipped them off to the Kent-Wolkoff connection. When detectives began to investigate Kent's activities more closely, they discovered that Kent was the American Embassy leak.

Scotland Yard was going to arrest Anna Wolkoff anyway, because of her correspondence with Lord Haw Haw. But arresting Kent was another matter. There was fear that the United States would be outraged if a U.S. citizen were tried by a British court, which might damage chances of further American aid. This was nicely avoided by holding the trial in secret. (These fears were well founded. When a report of Kent's trial was made public in 1944, it produced a fairly heated anti-British outcry in the United States.)

There was also the matter of Kent's position at the American Embassy. As a member of the embassy staff, Kent was covered by diplomatic immunity.

There was a way around this, as well. When U.S. Ambassador Joseph P. Kennedy (the future president's father) was informed of what Kent had been doing with the embassy's secret communiqués, he dismissed Kent from the diplomatic staff. This put an end to his diplomatic immunity.

Ambassador Kennedy was so angry that he wished he could have had the young diplomat shot as a spy. From what is known about Kennedy and his attitude toward England, he was not angered over what Kent did to undermine British security. It was because Kent had embarrassed him and made him seem slipshod when it came to security at the embassy.

The ambassador telephoned President Roosevelt on the night of May 20, 1940—five days before the British Army's evacuation at Dunkirk. He told the president in an anguished voice that the State Department's "Gray Code" had been broken. This meant that until a new code could be implemented, the U.S. confidential communications system would have to be blacked out all over the world.

The break in communications could not have come at a worse time. The Germans were overrunning France. The British Army was being hemmed into a pocket on the Channel coast; the French army had all but collapsed. And the United States could not use its most secret code to get in touch with either country.

Anna Wolkoff was the first to be arrested, but Tyler Kent's arrest was more dramatic. On the morning of May 20, a man identifying himself as "Police" knocked on the door of Kent's flat. Kent refused to let the man in, and the door had to be forced open.

The authorities were taking no chances—the men who came to arrest Kent were two Scotland Yard detectives, an MI.5 officer, and a member of the U.S. Embassy staff. They brought a warrant to search the flat. They had come prepared for all eventualities.

In the flat, the police found copies and photos of 1,500 documents—every bit of correspondence received by the American Embassy during Kent's time in London. Also found were a duplicate key to the embassy code room and a key to the index files, as well as a box of Anna Wolkoff's "Jew's War" labels.

While the four men were going through Kent's flat, the telephone rang. It was picked up by a Scotland Yard man. On the other end, someone from the Italian Embassy said that the next diplomatic pouch would soon be leaving for Rome, and asked if the next "package" was ready. And so, by sheer luck, MI.5 found out about the Kent/Wolkoff Italian link.

With Kent's dismissal from the embassy, his diplomatic immunity ended and he could be tried by the British courts. His secret trial was held in October, after Anna Wolkoff had already been tried, found guilty, and sentenced to 10 years in prison. Throughout the trial, Kent insisted that he was not a spy, and that he had only been collecting evidence to prove that Franklin D. Roosevelt was conspiring to involve the United States in a war.

This argument fell on deaf ears. Kent was found guilty of obtaining secret documents, and of using them to undermine the safety of Britain. His sentence was seven years behind stone walls, specifically the stone walls of Camp Hill, on the Isle of Wight, which was a jail for political prisoners built around an old monastery.

Tyler Kent's argument that he was not a spy was probably true in the literal sense; that is to say, he was not an employee of the Abwehr or any other German agency. But Kent's actions, and the inability of Scotland Yard and MI.5 to discover the Kent/Wolkoff/Italian Embassy connection sooner, inflicted irreparable damage to Britain's military position in France, as well as to American prestige in the eyes of her allies.

After the war, high-ranking German officers testified to the value of Kent's information. They admitted that the stolen documents had given a detailed picture of the British Army's strength and deployment in France. Without Kent's reports to enlighten them, the General Staff never would have allowed themselves the luxury of staying behind their Siegfried Line fortifications during the "Phony War" in the winter of 1939–1940.

The Wehrmacht was able to use those winter months in preparation for its planned spring offensive, building up its forces without fear of an attack by British or French forces. German officers knew that the British Army lacked the men and equipment to mount any sort of attack and would not be making any aggressive moves—because Tyler Kent told them.

In May 1940, when the Wehrmacht broke out from behind its Siegfried defenses, German planners were able to launch their attack against the Low Countries and into France, where British forces were weakest—also because of intelligence supplied by Tyler Kent.

So MI.5's contention that no German agent remained at large in Britain has some accuracy in the case of Tyler Kent, since Kent was not a German agent. He was just a dedicated anti-Communist zealot, whose zeal was misguided and misplaced.

British counterintelligence forces did such a good job at covering up their mistakes that it is sometimes hard to tell where their smoke-screen ends and the truth begins. They claim that they caught and "turned" every German agent that came to Britain. They did capture many, and were lucky with others—such as Ter Brank, who conveniently killed himself. But even spies who were caught frequently managed to send useful reports to Germany before MI.5 got wise to them. In most cases, it is almost impossible to tell when an agent stopped being a genuine Abwehr spy and started working for "Double-X."

In the summer of 1940, after the Low Countries had been overrun and France had surrendered, the Abwehr was faced with the fact that its network had to be enlarged. Men and women from all over the Greater Reich—occupied Western Europe—were recruited as agents. Two of the Abwehr's newest recruits were a couple of young Norwegians named Jack Berg and Olav Klausen.

The two had the advantage of being fluent in English—Berg's grandfather lived in London, and Klausen had several British friends. They were also young, with a sense of adventure and no idea of what they were getting into, and would be glad to go to England as a sort of extended holiday. The Abwehr's promise that they would be well paid for their services made the prospect even more appealing. An assignment in England seemed not only exciting but profitable; they both agreed to go as Abwehr agents.

The first part of their plan consisted of spreading rumors of their intention to escape Norway. They began telling friends that they had every intention of taking a small boat to England, to get away from the hated Nazis. Abwehr contacts within the Norwegian underground also did their part, by making sure that the necessary people in the movement heard about the planned "escape."

While the rumors were making their appointed rounds, Berg and Klausen were being trained in the Abwehr's espionage methods—exercises in observing without being observed, in sending concise and factual reports, in learning and deciphering codes, in making invisible ink.

The were also instructed in sabotage methods by Abwehr experts. Berg was a willing enough pupil. But Klausen had been a sergeant in a Norwegian sapper unit and already knew all about handling demolition charges, the best place to plant explosives for knocking out a bridge, and how to go about knocking out a factory.

Both Klausen and Berg were loyal members of Vidkun Quisling's Norwegian Nazi Party and took their training more seriously than anyone who knew them might have expected. In the spring of 1941, after weeks of instruction, they were pronounced "ready" for their assignment, which was given the code name "Hummer III Nord." (Lobster III North).

At the end of April 1941, Berg and Klausen landed on the east coast of Scotland in the vicinity of Aberdeen. They had been flown in from Norway aboard an ungainly Blohm & Voss flying boat; from the seaplane, they paddled ashore in a rubber dinghy, along with two bicycles, a radio, and a supply of explosives.

On the day after they landed, they transmitted their first radio signal. Jack Berg tapped out the letters "X . . . Y . . . Z" on the Morse key—code for "Landed safely. Sending without interference." This was acknowledged at once by their contact in Oslo.

From the landing area, the two cycled to a spot just north of Glasgow, where they hid their bikes and buried their cache of explosives. They walked into Glasgow and took a train into London. On May 1, Col. von Lahousen noted in his diary: " The two agents sent to England in the course of Hummer III Nord have arrived successfully. They have reported from London with the special radio equipment they had taken with them."

Reports from "Jack and OK," as they were known in the Abwehr, became confused after this, as well as confusing and inaccurate. Maybe they should have paid more attention during the lectures on ship identification.

Jack Berg radioed that a large troop convoy had sailed from Liverpool, and the message was relayed to Germany. Berlin believed that the convoy must be headed toward Norway and spread the alarm. However, the convoy never materialized, off Norway or anywhere else. Berlin demanded an explanation, and the best one that Jack Berg could come up with was that the ships had returned to port, and that the sailing had only been an exercise.

The two Norwegians had better success with sabotage. They returned to Scotland, unearthed their supply of explosives, and went back south again to carry out their assignments.

"Jack and OK" sent word that they had been responsible for the fires and explosions that wrecked a munitions factory in southern England, as well as a food store. They also claimed to have blown up a lumberyard, which contained wood for the manufacture of aircraft frames. Col. von Lahousen was able to confirm these stories from reports in the British press, as well as from contacts in London.

Following their first fumbling attempts in England, "Jack and OK" became highly successful, both as spies and saboteurs. They kept blowing up strategic targets and objectives. The Luftwaffe flew sorties to drop them supplies, money, and explosives. In one instance, the Luftwaffe even staged an air raid to divert attention from one of their drops. This took place in Scotland in February 1943; the bombing attack killed a number of Scottish civilians.

Col. von Lahousen wasn't entirely satisfied with the glowing reports sent by the two Norwegians, however. Berg and Klausen were *too* successful, too effective to be true or believed. They seemed to be everywhere at once—blowing up valuable and strategic targets; sending reports on troop movements; all the while keeping Scotland Yard and MI.5 off balance. The colonel had the sinking feeling that MI.5 had got hold of them and their radio and had "turned" the pair. In other words, he thought that Berg and Klausen were now working for British counterintelligence, and that all their reports were false.

Col. von Lahousen was right in his suspicions. Or half right. MI.5 had turned Jack Berg into a double-agent. Olav Klausen would not go along with his partner, however, and was thrown into an internment camp. MI.5 had to come up with some excuse for

Klausen's disappearance from the air waves. So they told the Abwehr that he had been recalled into the Norwegian army-in-exile, and that his unit had been sent from England to Iceland. Klausen, the Abwehr was told, went with his unit.

Nobody in the Abwehr was ever able to prove that "Jack and OK" were actually double agents, or that their stories were fairy tales. But from early 1943 onward, Col. von Lahousen had little faith in any of their reports.

The two Norwegians did their share of damage while at large in Britain. But how much was real, and how much was MI.5 fiction? Which is to ask: When were Jack and OK actually caught by MI.5?

The Abwehr never knew for certain. And MI.5 wouldn't say, which probably means that Berg and Klausen caused more trouble than counterintelligence cared to admit.

Had MI.5 agents been able to detain the two shortly after they came ashore, they would have crowed about it from the rooftops—if not during the war, to keep the Germans guessing, then following a safe interval after May 1945. Their official silence betokens failure on their part, failure to have caught the two spies/saboteurs before they were able to carry out their assignments. Which has always been their claim regarding all enemy agents who came to Britain.

CHAPTER 6

Tip-Offs, Tales and Promises

• • • • •

FROM HER BEDROOM, 13-YEAR-OLD ROSEMARY COOKE COULD HEAR THE muffled throbbing of engines quite clearly; the noise seemed to be coming from somewhere out to sea. But because of the fog, she could not even see as far as the beach.

It was past midnight on June 13, 1942. Before she could open her window to look out, Rosemary had to turn her light off—in accordance with the blackout regulations along that part of the Atlantic coast. Although she couldn't see what was making the noise, Rosemary wasn't worried. There was a Coast Guard station at Amagansett, Long Island, just under a mile down the beach. The engines offshore probably had something to do with the Coast Guard.

The noise that Rosemary Cooke heard had nothing to do with the Coast Guard. She was hearing *U-202* switch over from electric motors, which Lindner was using for running close to shore because they were quieter, to the submarine's diesel engines. Now that he had landed his four-man party on the American coast, Lindner wanted his boat's more powerful diesels to take him out of U.S. waters as quickly as possible. Noise was no longer a main consideration; now, speed mattered more than stealth.

At that moment, George Dasch, Ernest Burger, and the other two members of their group were at work on the beach, burying the crates of plastic explosives and fuses they had unloaded from the submarine.

George Dasch had still not decided how to go about upsetting the sabotage operation. But Ernest Burger was already doing his best to uncover the landing, in the literal sense. Although he had been ordered to bring nothing of German origin ashore with him, Burger brought a number of things from *U-202*, and left them in plain sight on the beach—a packet of German cigarettes; a half-filled bottle of liquor. He also left a trail of clothes along the sand, including a cap with the Kriegsmarine insignia on it, as well as a spade and a sea bag. The trail helped searchers find the explosives.

A short distance from where Rosemary Cooke sat by her bedroom window, Coastguardsman John Cullen was making his routine beach patrol from the Amagansett Coast Guard station. He had walked about a half-mile east of the station when he came across four men— Dasch and his three companions. One of the men, George Dasch himself, said that they were fishermen who had run aground. Cullen invited him to spend the rest of the night at the station, which would be a lot drier and warmer than waiting on the beach until sunrise.

Dasch's response came as a total surprise. "Forget about this," he told the Coastguardsman, "and I'll give you some money. You'll hear from me in Washington." He pressed into Cullen's hand, and said, "Take a good look at me." He wanted to be sure that Cullen would recognize him again.

"What is your name, boy?" Dasch asked.

"Frank Collins," the coastguardsman replied, and began running back to the station to report the incident.

Dasch had been instructed to overpower or kill any such intruder. Instead, he deliberately aroused the coastguardsman's suspicions, his first act in revealing the plot.

Dasch had also saved John Cullen's life. Cullen was going to walk past Dasch toward the other three members of Dasch's team. Heinrich Heinck and Richard Quirin would certainly have tried to kill the coastguardsman if Dasch hadn't sent him away with the $260. As it was, Heinck and Quirin wanted to know why Dasch hadn't killed him, as he had been ordered to do.

After burying the crates, Dasch, Burger, Quirin, and Heinck walked off the beach, and found their way to the railway station. They still had no real idea of where they were. Dasch found out when he saw the "AMAGANSETT" station sign. Which meant that they had landed a few miles off course—a short distance down the beach. But, considering the fog, Lindner had not done a bad job of navigating.

From Amagansett, the four men took a train to Jamaica, Queens. In Jamaica, they split up—Heinrich Heinck and Richard Quirin went off on their own; Dasch and Ernest Burger took a train into Manhattan together.

When he registered at the Governor Clinton Hotel, just adjacent Pennsylvania Station, Dasch used his cover name: "George John Day." He was tempted to use his real name, but Ernest Burger was standing right next to him. He still didn't know Burger's feelings toward their sabotage mission and did not want to take any chances.

Dasch had made a few clumsy attempts to find out Burger's state of mind while they were still on board *U-202*, but Dasch had an annoying tendency to talk too much when he was under a strain, and aboard the submarine, he was under constant strain. His rambling attempts at conversation only served to irritate Burger. Instead of coaxing him to talk, Dasch only needled Burger into silence.

The two of them spent their first day in Manhattan by visiting all the tourist attractions, including Radio City Music Hall. Dasch knew the city very well, from prewar days, and even dropped in on some of his old waiter friends. He did a lot of bragging; for one thing, he told his former boss that he would be reading all about his exploits in the newspapers fairly soon.

Most of this was just more nervous chatter on Dasch's part, complete with jokes and back-slapping all round. But someone made a remark that Dasch would remember later on: Some big shot in Washington might get all the information he could out of Dasch, and then leave him completely on his own. "Be careful," he was warned. But Dasch dismissed the idea. He knew that nothing like that could ever happen in the United States.

Second Lieutenant John Murdock, U.S. Army Signal Corps, was in command of the radar station at Montauk Point, on the extreme eastern tip of Long Island. The men at the radar station had a deal with the coastguardsmen at Amagansett—the Coast Guard would let the Army use their shower facilities, and the Army agreed to come to the Coast Guard's assistance if called.

On the morning of June 13, Lt. Murdock received a phone call from Amagansett. Some people had landed by rubber boat a few hours earlier and tried to bribe a coastguardsman on beach patrol, he was told. Lt. Murdock went down to see what the trouble was.

At Amagansett, Lt. Murdock was shown several boxes that had been unearthed, as well as some odds and ends of clothes. But the people who had left them there had long since vanished. Since there was nothing for him to do at Amagansett, Lt. Murdock drove back to Montauk Point.

On his second day in the United States, George Dasch decided to force the issue with Ernest Burger. He called Burger into his hotel room, locked the door, and told him that only one of them would leave the room alive if they did not reach an agreement.

Dasch asked Burger point blank about his opinion of Operation Pastorius and the sabotaging of American factories and railways. Burger's answer came as a complete surprise.

He wanted nothing to do with any sabotage operation, he said, and also said he thought Dasch was an American agent!

He had only agreed to take part in Operation Pastorius to get away from the secret police, the Gestapo; he was afraid that the Gestapo might try to arrest him if he stayed in Germany. Because Dasch had not reported Burger's outburst against the Gestapo, which he made while they were both still at Quenzsee, Burger had concluded that Dasch must be employed by the Americans in some secret fashion.

Dasch was greatly relieved to hear this. He corrected Burger's false impression that he was actually an American agent, and said that he was going to report Operation Pastorius to the FBI—he had apparently made his mind up since he had arrived in Manhattan. Burger went along with the idea—"I'm with you 100 percent!" is what he said, according to Dasch.

It would be best to report to the FBI in person, Dasch thought, and he made plans to go to Washington, D.C. But he wanted to wait a few days before he went. For one thing, he wanted to wait until the second group of saboteurs landed in Florida. Also, he wanted to see if a member of the Florida group, Herbert Hans Haupt, would join Burger and himself in their plan to destroy Operation Pastorius. He wanted "to give Haupt a chance to show his true colors, too." Haupt had grown up in the United States and was an American citizen.

Burger didn't argue these points, but he did suggest that Dasch contact the FBI office in New York as soon as possible, and the sooner the better. He could telephone the New York office to inform the bureau about the operation and indicate that he would be going to

FBI headquarters in a day or two to make a full report. It sounded like a good idea to Dasch.

From a pay telephone, Dasch phoned the FBI's Manhattan office after dinner. Burger waited outside the booth.

The conversation was a curious one. Dasch told the federal agent who answered the phone, Agent Dean McWhorter, that he had a "message of importance," and asked the agent's name. McWhorter refused to identify himself. This rattled Dasch, and put him on the defensive—Walter Kappe had warned that Gestapo agents had infiltrated the FBI. And Burger's tales of the Gestapo didn't help to steady his nerves.

Dasch decided that he had better not give his name, either. He told McWhorter that his name was Franz Daniel Pastorius and that he had landed from a German submarine the day before, along with three other men. McWhorter asked Dasch to come around to his office and tell him all about it—he obviously didn't believe a word of Dasch's story.

But Dasch had no intention of coming to see McWhorter. He was determined to make his report to J. Edgar Hoover, in Washington. He did ask McWhorter to pass their conversation along to FBI headquarters, and to add that Franz Daniel Pastorius would be appearing in person within a few days to give full particulars.

Dean McWhorter did make an official note that "F.D. Pastorius" had telephoned, and had informed the agent that he had just arrived from Germany. But he did not pass the information or the fact that "Postorius" had telephoned, along to FBI headquarters in Washington.

After making the phone call to McWhorter, Dasch seemed to have lost all track of time. He got involved in a card game with his waiter friends, a marathon session that lasted a day and a half. Dasch later said that he left for Washington on June 17. But records show that he did not take the train from Pennsylvania Station until the 18th. He was either so involved with his game that he forgot what day it was, or was so nervous that time got away from him.

Before he got on the train, Dasch put $80,000 of Operation Pastorius expense money into a new brief case, along with $4,000 from his money belt. Burger was also on hand while this was being done. The hotel staff had already reserved a room for Dasch at Washington's Hotel Mayflower.

Dasch did not particularly want to see the other two members of his group before he left for Washington. He was not overly fond of either Heinrich Heinck or Richard Quirin, and was especially put off by Quirin's unpleasant manner—Quirin still thought that *he* should have been the leader of the Pastorius mission.

At about 7 P.M. on June 18, a Thursday, George Dasch arrived in Washington, and went straight to his hotel. Ernest Burger stayed behind in New York, waiting for something to happen.

While George Dasch was still playing cards in New York, Edward Kerling's group of saboteurs were landing on the Florida coast. On the night of June 17, submarine *U-584* delivered Kerling and his three companions, Werner Thiel, Herbert Hans Haupt, and Hermann Neubauer, to Ponte Vedra, on the Atlantic coast and a few miles from the city of Jacksonville.

No Coast Guard patrol stumbled across Kerling's landing. The four men came ashore completely undetected. They buried the boxes of fuses and explosives on the beach, just as Dasch and his party had done, and headed inland. Kerling realized that he would have a lot to do within the next few days.

The first thing Kerling wanted to take care of came under the heading of "personal matters." He had plans to divorce his wife, who was employed as a cook in New York, and marry Hedy Engemann, who worked in her family's Yorkville grocery store. These arrangements were in addition to putting his part of Operation Pastorius in motion.

Herbert Haupt and Hermann Neubauer were sent off to Chicago, on separate trains, to await instructions. Kerling and Werner Thiel took a train to New York, via Cincinnati, to shake off any possible police shadow. Actually, Kerling had no real fear of being detected by police; going by way of Cincinnati was only a precaution.

Kerling's main concern wasn't the police or the FBI; it was how to get the explosives off the beach at Ponte Vedra. Wartime restrictions made travel inconvenient; buying gasoline required a government-issued coupon and restricted the buyer to a certain amount. And lugging crates of explosives on and off trains, or through the countryside, would be certain to arouse suspicion. For the time being, it was safest to leave the crates buried in the sand.

When Kerling reached New York, he took a train out to Astoria, on Long Island, to visit a friend from prewar days. Besides being

Kerling's friend, Helmut Leiner was also a member of the German-American Bund, the Nazi Party's American branch, as well as a bona fide Abwehr contact. Leiner's name and address were given to George Dasch and the other Pastorius members, written in invisible ink on a handkerchief. Walter Kappe had included his name on a listing of sympathetic parties to be contacted in case of trouble. Kerling wanted to recruit Leiner's help in moving the cache of explosives from Florida.

Kerling also began making arrangements for his divorce, as well as arrangements with Hedy Engemann, through Helmut Leiner. Leiner was acquainted with both women, and was known by people in the community. He would be able to contact lawyers and perform other delicate matters without being noticed, while a stranger, especially a foreigner, might arouse curiosity.

Kerling and Leiner went to Newark, New Jersey, for help in moving the explosives from Florida. They had the address of a pro-Nazi pastor there, and hoped that the man might be of assistance. But when they got to Newark, they could not find their pastor and read that he had been arrested. They had the name and address of another contact in Philadelphia, also a pro-Nazi churchman; it might be worth while to go to Philadelphia for a word with him.

Those packing crates in Florida were causing more of a problem than Kerling had anticipated. But still, he had no reason to worry. He was not scheduled to meet with George Dasch until early July, which was more than two weeks away. The bomb-making explosives ought to be moved to a safe place by then, or at least some sort of plan for getting them off the beach should be made.

But apart from the explosives, Kerling could not foresee any difficulties. The landing from the U-Boat had not been detected; he and his three men had traveled many hundreds of miles within the United States without arousing the slightest suspicion. He could see no reason at all why Operation Pastorius should not accomplish everything it was supposed to.

After a night's sleep in Washington, George Dasch telephoned the U.S. Government Information Service from his room at the Mayflower Hotel. Even though he had been in touch with the FBI in New York, now he was not certain where he should go to tell his story. Army Intelligence, or G-2, which was roughly the Abwehr's equivalent, might be more appropriate than the FBI.

The girl at the Information Service who answered the telephone suggested that Dasch contact a Colonel H. F. Kramer, of the army's General Staff Corps. Dasch took this advice and telephoned Kramer, but the colonel was not in his office at the time. Dasch left a message with Kramer's secretary, who promised that the colonel would return the call as soon as he returned.

After half an hour's wait and no call from Col. Kramer, Dasch's nerves got the better of him. He dialed the FBI.

He told the federal agent basically the same thing he had told Dean McWhorter in New York—he was the leader of eight men who had landed in the United States. Dasch also referred to his conversation with McWhorter. Because McWhorter had not informed Washington of the conversation, the federal agent at FBI headquarters, Duane L. Traynor (nicknamed "Pie" Traynor, after the baseball star of the 1920s), had no idea what Dasch was talking about.

Traynor suggested that Dasch come down to headquarters and say what was on his mind. Because Dasch said that he did not know Washington very well, and did not know where FBI headquarters was, Traynor sent someone to the hotel to pick him up.

While waiting for the FBI to arrive, Col. Kramer finally telephoned. After hearing Dasch's story, Kramer suggested that Dasch come and talk to him right away. But Dasch told the colonel that the FBI was already on the way over. Shortly after he put down the phone, someone from FBI headquarters came to take Dasch to see Pie Traynor.

After talking to the FBI for a while, Dasch probably wished he had gone to see Col. Kramer instead. He could see that nobody believed a word he had said. He told Pie Traynor and another agent, named Ladd, that he had landed by rubber boat on Long Island, and that he had been sent to disrupt America's coal and light metals industry. The federal agents just looked at him with blank expressions.

Dasch was under a great deal of strain, and his story was becoming more rambling and incoherent each time he told it. He said that he felt that it was his duty as a former soldier of the U. S. Army to foil Operation Pastorius, and insisted that the matter could only be reported to J. Edgar Hoover himself. The more Dasch talked, the more skeptical the two agents became.

Nobody bothered to examine the suitcase he brought with him, or even to ask about it. Since he was getting nowhere, Dasch opened the case and dumped its contents—$84,000 in cash—all over the table. Traynor and Ladd, to put it mildly, were astonished.

A bit carried away, Dasch shouted that it was a Nazi present, "from the black of the party's heart and soul!" Along with all the money, which overflowed the table and had spilled onto the floor, was a note: "This money I took from Hitler in the hope that it would be used toward his defeat." It was signed: George John Dasch.

The two federal agents finally began to believe his story.

When the Federal Bureau of Investigation decided to listen to George Dasch, they listened with an intensity that made up for their initial skepticism. For the next eight days, federal agents interrogated him. Military Intelligence also asked their share of questions. His testimony was taken down by stenographers working in relay; it ran over 260 pages.

Dasch was questioned about items besides Operation Pastorius. He was asked about the use of Irish nationals against Britain (but not about the IRA in the United States—the FBI had apparently not known about IRA sabotage in New Jersey and other places); the rumored enlistment of Soviet prisoners of war into a German army unit called "Free Russia"; as well as other sabotage campaigns against both the United States and Britain.

He told what he knew, although his information on most of these topics was usually sketchy. One subject he was able to discuss at length was the "spy school" at Quenzsee and Abwehr training methods. Another was the submarine base at Lorient, as well as what he had learned about U-Boats while crossing the Atlantic aboard *U-202*.

Sometimes, he would ramble nervously. He mentioned Rudolph Hess' flight to Scotland in May 1941; his wife's internment, and any number of things that had no bearing on the subject at hand. His interrogators listened impatiently, and always managed to come up with still more questions.

Most important to the federal agents was the whereabouts of the other Pastorius agents. Here, Dasch was more than eager to answer any and all questions; he might even have been overeager, at least to the FBI's way of thinking. He wanted to take part in the arrests, to act as "finger man" for the accompanying federal agents, which he thought would be the surest way to identify the other saboteurs. But the bureau finally talked him out of that, and Dasch told them what they wanted to know about the other seven men.

Ernest Burger, Dasch's fellow anti-saboteur, was in Manhattan. Federal agents had no trouble locating him. They found him in his room at the Governor Clinton Hotel, right where Dasch said he would be.

Information supplied by Dasch was instrumental in the capture of the other two men in his group. Heinrich Heinck and Richard Quirin were arrested in Manhattan, picked up on the street. Quirin was apprehended in front of a tailor's shop, Heinck after he left a delicatessen.

Ernest Burger's help resulted in the tracing, and subsequent arrest, of Edward Kerling and Werner Thiel. Burger had given detailed descriptions of the two men, which proved invaluable. They were both arrested in Manhattan, along with Kerling's friend Helmut Leiner.

The last of the Pastorius saboteurs were picked up on June 27—just 10 days after they had landed in Florida. Herbert Haupt and Hermann Neubauer were arrested in Chicago. Dasch had not known their exact whereabouts, but had given descriptions of the two, as well as possible destinations that Haupt and Neubauer might have chosen after coming ashore. The FBI was provided with a place to start looking, as well as a picture of the faces of who they were looking for.

Without Dasch's help, as well as Ernest Burger's, the FBI would never have arrested any of the Operation Pastorius agents. Or at least not until they sabotaged one of the Alcoa plants, or blew up a railway locomotive. And possible not even then. The bureau never did find out who blew up the Hercules Powder plant in New Jersey, let alone arrest anybody. Any damage done to aluminum plants or railway stock would probably have been "officially" noted as having been caused by accidents or negligence.

The explosives that had been buried on the beach at Ponte Vedra were unearthed before Haupt and Neubauer had been arrested. After his arrest, Edward Kerling had taken federal agents to the burial spot, which was marked by three palm tree stumps, and watched as the four boxes were unearthed. With this, and the arrest of all the Pastorius agents, the FBI had everyone and everything connected with Operation Pastorius in its custody.

Now that the sabotage operation had been destroyed, George Dasch worried about his part in the matter. His main concern was over his mother and relatives in Germany. If anyone in Berlin found out that he had been responsible for the demise of Operation Pastorius, Dasch feared that the Gestapo would arrest his family. Once members of his family were in custody, Walter Kappe might think up something nasty for them. Kappe was just the type.

Federal agents Traynor and Ladd assured Dasch that his part in the break-up of Operation Pastorius would be kept secret, and that his picture would not be used. In fact, he was told that the bureau wanted the Abwehr to think that the sabotage operation had been discovered by the FBI alone, without any outside help, and that neither Dasch's name nor his picture would appear in connection with the capture of the other men. This was to discourage the Abwehr from trying the same thing again in the near future, or at least that was what Dasch was told.

The two agents also asked Dasch if he would continue to cooperate with them, even though the other six men were in custody. What they wanted him to do was show up in prison, where the six captive saboteurs were being held. Some of the six refused to answer the FBI's questions; apparently, they thought that Dasch was still at large. But if they could see that he was behind bars, as well, the six would see that the game was up and would be more willing to talk. This made sense to Dasch. He agreed to play along with them.

Dasch was taken to New York on July 28, the day after Haupt and Neubauer were arrested in Chicago. He was placed under formal arrest at the Federal Court Building, although nobody bothered to tell him that he had been arrested.

In the court building, he was given a prison uniform, photographed with a prison number, "and generally put through the arrest routine." All of this was just part of the act to convince the other men, he was told. Finally, he was led past the cells of all the other Pastorius men, except Burger, so that everybody could see him, and put in a cell by himself. Agents Traynor and Ladd continued to assure him that everything would be all right.

While he was alone in his cell, Dasch happened to look through the opening in the door. He couldn't see very far or very much. But he did see a guard just outside, reading a copy of the New York *Daily News*; on the front page was his own picture, under the headline: "CAPTURED NAZI SPY."

Alarmed by this, Dasch asked to see someone of authority. Agent Pie Traynor came to his cell, along with the agent in charge of the New York office, an agent named Donegan. They were both surprised that Dasch knew anything about the picture. Donegan was annoyed, and barked, "How the hell do you know that?"

But Traynor continued to reassure Dasch. He explained that Dasch would be put on trial with the other saboteurs "in order to fool the Nazis." Within six months, however, after all the excitement had blown over, he would be released with a full presidential pardon, and completely exonerated of all charges on which he would be tried. Traynor made this promise in the name of Attorney General Francis C. Biddle, as well as FBI Director J. Edgar Hoover.

Traynor was convincing. He also persuaded Dasch that he should plead guilty to charges of sabotage—it would keep his part in the foiling of Operation Pastorius away from the Nazis, he was told. He didn't like the idea of pleading guilty, since he explained that he never had any intention of committing any acts of sabotage. But he agreed to go along with the FBI's plan.

Dasch was feeling uneasy about everything he had seen and heard since he turned himself in to the FBI. Three or four days after he had seen his photo in the *Daily News*, his uneasiness turned to alarm. He was presented with the charges against him: illegal entry into United States; planned sabotage against the United States; espionage; conspiracy; and other lesser charges. He was further informed that he would be tried by a secret military tribunal. Traynor had said that his trial would take place in a civil court.

This last item especially rattled Dasch. He asked to speak with agent Donegan, who was in charge of the New York office. Donegan said that he didn't know anything about any "deal" between Dasch and the FBI; Dasch would be put on trial for his life. Having straightened out his prisoner, Donegan started for the door.

Before Donegan could get outside, Dasch shouted that he was changing his plea from "guilty" to "not guilty." His outburst did not seem to have any effect; Donegan did not stop to discuss the matter, or even to break his stride.

On the following day, Dasch, Burger, and the other six Pastorius members were transferred to the federal prison in Washington, D.C. Each of the eight men was kept in a separate cell and was under armed guard by the U.S. Army. None was allowed any visitors.

The shouting incident with Donegan in New York must have been reported. Dasch was in Washington only a few days when a guard came to escort him from his cell to a large room inside the prison. There, he met an assembly of the highest legal and law enforcement authorities in the country: J. Edgar Hoover; Attorney General Francis Biddle; the U.S. Army's judge advocate general, Major General Myron C. Cramer; the army provost marshal of Washington, D.C., Brigadier General Albert L. Cox; and several other men of importance.

The meeting had been convened to coax Dasch to change his plea back to "guilty." "We want you to plead guilty," Attorney General Biddle said, "to speed up the trial."

Biddle and J. Edgar Hoover both told Dasch that they knew he was not guilty, but everyone insisted that he plead guilty to all charges; it would expedite matters.

Dasch wanted to know if the arrangement with agent Traynor was still in effect. Attorney General Biddle didn't seem to know what he was talking about, but Hoover said, "Oh, yes, it all stands."

Because of Biddle's reaction, Dasch asked Hoover to be more specific about the government's part in the bargain—and if he was still to receive a full presidential pardon within six months. Hoover was in no mood to haggle. He curtly repeated that "it all stands" and wouldn't say any more.

Both Hoover and Attorney General Biddle were quite intent on having Dasch plead guilty. Biddle asked him repeatedly to change his plea. Hoover even paid Dasch a personal visit, in the prisoner's cell, to try his hand at convincing him.

But Dasch insisted that he was *not* guilty. He had committed no crime against the United States and had never intended to take part in any sabotage operation. He had been more than willing to cooperate with the authorities, as long as there was going to be a civil trial, held in public. But not if there was to be a military trial, held in secret. He especially distrusted the fact that the trial had to be in secret—there was already too much secrecy connected with the government's motives to suit him.

Dasch was not satisfied with the excuse that his guilty plea would "speed up" the trial. It seemed awfully flimsy—asking him to say that he had plotted against the United States, to lie and put his life on the line, just so the proceedings could end a day or two early.

It also seemed that Hoover was holding something back. It was as though he wanted something, but would not say what.

What J. Edgar Hoover wanted was to make himself look efficient and aggressive. And he wanted to do it at George Dasch's expense.

Hoover and the Federal Bureau of Investigation had been riding the crest of the wave in the 1920s and 1930s, but lately their stock had fallen off. In the decade before the war started, "G-men" captured or killed a number of bank robbers and criminals, frequently in well-publicized gun battles. These stakeouts sometimes went wrong, and innocent bystanders were killed in the resulting shootouts, but these glaring errors were never mentioned to the public by the press.

The tracking down and killing of John Dillinger, "Public Enemy Number One," probably received the most publicity for both the FBI and J. Edgar Hoover. The Dillinger shooting helped make Hoover's reputation as the country's top law enforcement official.

But since the beginning of the war in 1939, Hoover had been under a cloud. He had been accused of misconduct in handling investigations of suspected left-wing sympathizers and of using "Gestapo tactics." He was also criticized for spending too much time in nightclubs. A Congressman called Hoover a "Stork Club detective," which was quoted in national newspapers. If the public had known about enemy sabotage in the United States, including the Hercules Powder factory incident, opinion of Hoover would have taken a dramatic tumble.

As it was, there were many in the country who were saying that the great J. Edgar Hoover was not the man he used to be—he wasn't as sharp or effective and had gone soft since the glory days of the 1930s. Needless to say, a man with Hoover's ego didn't appreciate these rumors, and set out to stop them.

To show that he and his bureau were just as vigilant and efficient as they had been in the days of the Dillinger shootout, Hoover meant to take full credit for the capture of the Pastorius saboteurs. He was going to use the Pastorius incident to show the country that there was no need to fear as long as he and his boys were on the job; the nation was safe under the protection of the FBI, with Hoover in charge. Which meant, of course, that he was not about to share any credit with George Dasch. Not only would this make Dasch seem heroic—one man against Hitler—but, even worse, would make

Hoover look like he needed help from outsiders to do his job.

The idea of trying Dasch, Burger, and the other six by secret military court had not been Hoover's; it was Attorney General Biddle's. But Hoover was more than willing to go along with the idea.

It was a legal, but rare, procedure to try civilians under the rules of a court-martial. The last civilians to be tried by military tribunal were the conspirators in Abraham Lincoln's assassination in 1865. A military trial would make things more difficult for Dasch and Burger—and easier for Hoover. Under military law, the accused is presumed to be guilty until proven innocent. The burden of proof would be upon Dasch and Burger, and Hoover would see to it that the burden would be an impossible one.

Throughout the country, there was little doubt whether or not Dasch and Burger were guilty. According to what Americans read in the newspapers, the two were "Nazi spies" and ought to be put to death. A *Life* magazine headline captured the public mood: "The Eight Nazi Saboteurs Should Be Put to Death."

J. Edgar Hoover was a national hero, just as he had planned. And Dasch and Burger were just two more Nazis, also as Hoover had planned. The country demanded a return to frontier-style justice—give the bastards a fair trial, and then hang them!

This outlook was not confined to the man in the street. President Franklin D. Roosevelt, who was commander-in-chief of the U.S. armed forces and had authorized the military trial, asked an aide what should be done about the men—"Should they be shot or hanged?"

CHAPTER 7

Teuto-Brasileiro

• • • • •

S OME OF THE MOST EFFECTIVE AGENTS IN GERMAN INTELLIGENCE, AND who did the most damage to both the British and Americans, did not operate in either Britain or the United States. The Abwehr agents who were in the best position to keep track of British and American shipping and convoys, as well as naval activities, were based in South America.

But besides observing merchant vessels and warships, which would have justified their existence by itself, these agents also relayed radio messages from agents within the United States to Berlin, and also kept the Abwehr well informed of Allied military strength in the Caribbean Sea and the South Atlantic. All in all, these were highly useful and productive agents. And neither the Federal Bureau of Investigation nor MI.5 could do anything about them.

Radio experts in Tirpitz Ufer had discovered an amazing phenomenon—short-wave signals traveled with less atmospheric interference and were received more clearly, when sent north-to-south as opposed to east-to-west. This technical discovery meant that it would be far simpler for Berlin to communicate with agents in South America than with agents inside the United States. Information on both military and industrial activities in the United States, and especially on shipping between the United States and Britain, was vitally important. So a secret radio link between the United States and Germany, with signals sent via South America, was a highly useful method of communication.

What made this method even more attractive was the fact that the Abwehr had a network of ready-made agents in place since before the war. Both Brazil and Argentina had communities of influential German immigrants, made up of individuals anxious to be of service to the Fatherland.

Between 1884 and 1941, roughly 200,000 Germans came to Brazil to improve their standard of living. By the outbreak of the war, nearly 900,000 Brazilians were either German-born or of German descent (Teuto-Brasileiro). In some towns, one out of every six Brazilians was of German blood. In some places, the ratio was one in four. Most of these had resisted assimilation and maintained strong ties, both cultural and emotional, with the Old Country.

When Admiral Canaris arranged to have German embassies used as "control points" for espionage activities, in the 1930s, the Rio de Janeiro embassy was one of the first chosen.

As soon as the war broke out, the Abwehr prepared to make use of its ready-made intelligence network in Brazil. Canaris and his staff realized that Brazil was of strategic importance. Agents in Brazil could give Naval High Command a clear picture of both British and American shipping in South American waters, as well as the Caribbean.

The northeastern hump of Brazil, which juts out into the Atlantic, was of particular importance. Admiral Jonas Ingram, commander of the U.S. Navy's "neutrality patrol" in the South Atlantic, called Cape Sao Roque "the most vital strategic point in the South American area." Cape Sao Roque is the western most point of Brazil, bringing it close to trans-Atlantic trade routes.

Also, the ports of Rio de Janeiro, Santos, and Recife were midway stations for British convoy routes. Agents in northeast Brazil could be of extreme value to U-Boats just by keeping their eyes open.

The political attitudes in Brazil, Argentina, and other South American countries also proved highly beneficial for the Abwehr.

While the war was going well for Germany, politicians were willing to look the other way when it came to German espionage. The President of Brazil, Getulio Vargas, was officially neutral. He declared his "entire solidarity" with the United States in the cause of hemisphere defense, and gave other words of encouragement to the U.S. State Department.

But he also gave his assurance to the German minister in Rio de Janeiro, Ambassador Pruter, that Brazil would not be delivered to the American camp. Brazil received arms from Germany, and Vargas allowed German agents to operate from Rio de Janeiro, Sao Paulo, and elsewhere in Brazil.

One high-ranking German official rated President Vargas' regime "the bulwark against the inclusion of South America in Roosevelt's anti-German policy." In spite of pledges of "solidarity," President Vargas wanted to be on the right side when the war was over. And in 1940, it looked like a sure thing that Germany would run away with it.

One of Germany's best men in Brazil was Albrecht Gustav Engels, who was an engineer by profession. Engels had been born in Germany, and served in the German army in 1914–1918. During the economic turmoil of the 1920s, he decided to emigrate to Brazil.

His job as chief engineer with German General Electric took him to major commercial and industrial centers in Brazil, where he made many connections in business, military, and even political circles. As Engels put it, he had "personal relations with a series of officers and society figures."

In the spring of 1939, Engels was enlisted into the Abwehr as a "V-Mann," a spy. He was a stable family man, just the opposite of the flashy and glamorous agents in spy novels. He was also well respected and, having lived 16 years in Brazil, had the contacts to provide a great deal of very useful information. Proud to be of assistance to his native country, Engels felt it his patriotic duty to provide any information that Berlin might request. His code-name was "Alfredo."

Engels sent information on industrial and military production in the United States, most of which was obtained from American technical journals, as well as news of U.S. trade with Brazil, and the rest of Latin America. This was just the beginning of his career in espionage. At this stage, his only means of communication was by mail; Engels sent his reports to Berlin via Rome, written in code.

After France surrendered in the spring of 1940, the Abwehr intensified its efforts in South America. Albrecht Engels was promoted; he became the center of the Abwehr's spy network in the Western Hemisphere. Agents in the United States would send their reports to Engels, who would then send them on to Berlin. He would also act as paymaster to these agents.

The assistant naval attaché in the German Embassy in Rio, Captain Hermann Bohny, would provide Engels with the money to run the organization. Bohny would also arrange the use of the diplomatic pouch and cable, for transporting agents' reports. Safe addresses were also arranged as "postal drops," places where agents in the United States and in South America could send their reports. Engels had been using his company's address—Post Office Box 100—but was afraid that its constant use might invite suspicion.

The letters Engels received concerned the production of aircraft and munitions in the United States, as well as shipping movements between the United States and Britain. Shipping information included routes, cargoes, armaments, size of crews, sometimes the names of individual ships, and their captains. Reports were written either in code or in secret ink, and were signed with code names: "Harry," "Fred," or "James."

Urgent reports needing immediate attention, such as convoy sailings, were sent via diplomatic cable. Officers at U-Boat Command had to have the information at once, if they were to intercept the convoys in midocean. Everything else was still sent by mail. The use of the microdot—photographing reports and reducing them to the size of a typewritten period—was a great innovation. Many microdot reports could be sent on a single sheet of paper and, because their size made it impossible to read them without specialized equipment, it became unnecessary to send the reports in code.

But the biggest improvement in communications came with the establishment of a radio station in Brazil, which relayed reports from agents in the United States to operators in Berlin. The station was given the code-name "Bolivar." The FBI eventually found out about the reports being sent to "Bolivar" from New York, Baltimore, Los Angeles, and other places in the United States, but apparently could not locate the senders. At any rate, the FBI was not able to stop the messages being sent.

Engels recruited more informants for his network, most of whom were also German immigrants. Most of the Abwehr requests for information concerned ship movements between American ports and Britain. Sometimes, other information was thrown in as well, free of charge.

One of Engels' men was able to obtain information on HMS *Birmingham* from drunken members of the British cruiser's crew. Another informant reported that the freighter *Robin Grey* was ready to depart for Africa, carrying, among other things, tanks, automatic weapons, and munitions.

The construction of airfields in northeastern Brazil by Pan American Airways was another of Engels' objectives—these airfields might be put to use as bases for anti-U-Boat patrols in the future. Any American activities involving aircraft or air bases was of vital interest to both the Abwehr and Admiral Dönitz, who was in command of all U-Boat operations.

Just as important were the activities of the U.S. South Atlantic Fleet. The American fleet, called the "neutrality patrol," operated out of Recife under the command of Adm. Ingram. Consisting of four light cruisers and five destroyers, the fleet patrolled the South Atlantic area between Trinidad, Cape Sao Roque, and the Cape Verde Islands. The regime of President Vargas allowed the Americans to use Recife and Salvador for supplies and repairs.

Albert Engels' espionage activities were not confined to convoys and the U.S. fleet. One of Berlin's more unusual requests involved the output of weapons-grade uranium in the United States. Engels received several typewritten sheets, filled with questions on firms in the United States that refined uranium: how much uranium ore these firms had and how they processed it. In short, the Abwehr wanted to know how far the United States had progressed with its atomic bomb program. It is not known how much Engels was able to find out from Brazil, but it probably was not very much.

Nor was Albert Engels' network the only spy setup in Brazil. A second organization was run by Friedrich Kempter. Kempter's life had followed the same basic pattern as Engels'—born in Germany; moved to Brazil during the economic chaos in Germany during the 1920s; recruited by the Abwehr shortly after the war broke out in 1939. The only minor difference was that Kempter became a spy for the money more than for patriotism and had not been directly recruited into the Abwehr. He had been offered money in return for information on shipping movements, from Rio de Janeiro, but the offer came from what appeared to be a Norwegian firm in Hamburg. Kempter, however, had more than a fair idea where his reports were really going.

In February 1940, Kempter established what seemed to be a commercial information bureau. He founded it with another German, a man named Herbert Müller and called the firm Rapid Information Ltd. The bureau was actually nothing more than a cover for Kempter's spy activities. Herr Müller did not know about Kempter's espionage business at first, but readily agreed to come into it when he found out.

The Abwehr's Hamburg branch was more than satisfied with Kempter's work. One Abwehr officer noted, in November 1940, that Kempter's reports "have been consistently accurate." These reports were sent to Hamburg either via air mail or cable. They covered topics such as the movement of British warships in Brazilian waters; American military activities in Latin America; convoy departures and arrivals, with notes on the cargoes of various freighters; and an occasional report on Brazilian internal politics, to assure Berlin that President Vargas was still officially "neutral."

Under instructions from Hamburg, Kempter also made contact with German agents in Argentina, as well as Ecuador. The Ecuador connection was especially important—that agent had a man keeping an eye on U.S. Naval activities in the Panama Canal Zone. His reports on Panama were relayed to Germany through Kempter.

Many of the Panama Canal reports concerned activities of the American armed services—the U.S. Navy was building a submarine base on the Pacific side, and the Army was setting up new camps and building new roads; the entire Canal Zone was bristling with "stupendous activity." Other reports covered British naval patrols in the area.

For two years, Kempter sent out a steady stream of reports. By December 1941, he had sent more than 400 radio messages, in addition to an unknown number of air mail messages. Hamburg acknowledged these reports and replied with more than 200 messages. Kempter's information was of such value that the Abwehr presented him with the War Service Cross, First Class.

Much of Kempter's invaluable data concerned British convoys and was sent on the personal request of Admiral Karl Dönitz, who wanted to know as much as possible about American shipping, particularly about American freighters or tankers that left Brazilian ports bound for England. Although the United States and Germany were not yet at war, relations between Berlin and Washington were deteriorating all throughout 1941. Dönitz wanted to be prepared.

But Kempter's convoy reports had a more immediate, and vital, use. In April 1940, just before the fall of France, the British Admiralty began rerouting its convoys to North Africa and the Mediterranean. Instead of going from England to North Africa via the

Straits of Gibraltar, shipping was being sent via the Suez Canal. The convoys would have to stop at Brazilian ports for more fuel and supplies before heading round the Cape of Good Hope, at the southern tip of Africa, and north to the Red Sea.

The "Gibraltar route" was more direct, but too many ships were being sunk before they ever got anywhere near their destination, which was usually the port of Tobruk. U-Boats were picking them off in mid-Atlantic. The Suez Canal route was the safer, although much longer, alternative.

Because of the hundreds of miles that were added on to the voyage, a stopping-off point would be needed for the convoys. Food, fresh water, and other supplies, as well as fuel oil, would have to be taken on somewhere along the way. Because of their location, Brazilian ports were the logical choice.

Dönitz also recognized the strategic value of Brazil. After France surrendered, U-Boats began operating from Brest and other Atlantic ports, which put them in a better position to intercept convoys heading to or coming from Brazil. Information on Allied ships in Brazilian ports became vital to Dönitz and his U-Boat captains—if given the sailing time of the convoys, the U-Boats could be in position to torpedo them.

Kempter's network, code-named the "King" organization, went to work supplying Dönitz with the data he needed. The Abwehr sent word that information on shipping bound for North Africa was "urgently desired." Field Marshal Erwin Rommel's Afrika Corps was pressing toward the Suez Canal; Rommel would be needing all the help he could get if he was to shatter the British Army, including help from the U-Boats to stop shipments of ammunition and supplies to the British.

In May 1941, Kempter was informed by one of his contacts that the British merchant ship *Rodney Star*, 12,000 tons, would be departing Buenos Aires for England. Kempter relayed the message to Germany. A few days later, the *Rodney Star* was sunk by a U-Boat.

At the end of May, "King" radioed Hamburg that a Norwegian ship was departing Buenos Aires. The Norwegian ship was also intercepted and sunk.

During the month of August, Kempter and one of his contacts, a German businessman named Karl Fink, kept a sharp watch on ship movements out of Rio de Janeiro and Recife. Kempter was able to report that merchantmen leaving the United States for the Middle East were stopping at Recife to refuel and resupply. From there, the convoys headed for St. Helena, a knob of rock in the middle of the South Atlantic, then around the Cape of Good Hope to the Providence Islands, where they refueled and re-supplied again before departing for the Red Sea and the Suez Canal.

Dönitz and his U-Boats made good use of Kempter's observations. Using information sent by Kempter, and other agents in South America and ports along the eastern United States, U-Boat wolf packs were able to intercept convoys in mid-Atlantic. The submarines knew in advance what convoys would be sailing, and could figure out the best point to make an interception.

During the first three months of 1941, when the "King" network began stepping up its activities to report on shipping movements from South American ports, more than 500,000 tons of shipping were sunk by U-Boats. This was an increase of nearly 1 million tons over the last three months of 1940, when 350,000 tons were sunk. Between March and June 1942, the number of tons increased again: 875,000 tons of Allied shipping were torpedoed.

Throughout 1941 and into 1942, Allied shipping losses continued at an alarming rate—500,000 tons per month, or more, were being sunk. Kempter and "King" were giving the Abwehr, and Dönitz, exactly the information they requested.

Hamburg's requests were keeping Kempter and his men busy throughout 1941. What made Kempter so valuable to the Abwehr was his ability to obtain information on both the British and the Americans.

Through his subagents and contacts, Friedrich Kempter was able to furnish the Abwehr section in Hamburg with accurate information on the antitorpedo netting used to protect British ships in Brazilian harbors, and even the thickness of the netting. He was also well connected enough to get his hands on the high- and low-tide tables for the English coast—highly useful information for putting spies ashore from a U-Boat. From his contacts in Panama, Kempter also sent information about British ships being routed through the Panama Canal.

Sub-agents in the United States sent Kempter a set of American navigation charts. He had a photographer friend take pictures of the charts; photos would be much easier to send to Germany than the awkward charts. He also sent photos of any Allied ships he was able to observe in Brazilian waters.

Kempter also received regular batches of cuttings from American magazines and newspapers, which he also sent along to Hamburg. Abwehr officials appreciated these news articles because of their "military, technical, and economic" value.

Not every Abwehr agent was as efficient as Albrecht Engels and Friedrich Kempter. Josef Starziczny, born in Germany and of Polish descent, came to Brazil in March 1941. Like Engels and Kempter, Starziczny set up a radio transmitter and, shortly after entering the country, established contact with Hamburg. His Abwehr contact was well pleased with the information he sent, and with the fact that he was setting up his own spy network.

The messages that Starziczny sent to Hamburg sometimes left a lot to be desired, though. One of his reports involved a fictitious story about a plot to overthrow Brazilian President Vargas by a pro-American clique. Starziczny heard rumors about such a plot and accepted the stories as fact. The Abwehr was fairly alarmed by the report, until Engels straightened out the story. No damage was done, except for a few gray hairs in Hamburg.

Sometimes, Starziczny's reports were accurate enough, but were not complete. He was not always able to find out the destination of British convoys sailing from Brazilian ports, or their sailing dates—which limited their use to U-Boat Command. And the reports were sometimes so vague that they were absolutely useless, such as a story about a naval battle between two warships which Starziczny did not bother to identify.

Because of his inefficiency, Starziczny was treated with resentment by Friedrik Kempter and some of his own contacts. Albrecht Engels told Hamburg that Starziczny wasted the Abwehr's time and money. Hamburg agreed, up to a point, and did not send as much money to Starziczny as to Kempter and Engels. Which meant that he was usually short of funds and could not always pay his agents and subagents on time. His contacts did not appreciate not being paid, which made them lax in their work and resulted in sloppy work and still more inaccurate reports to Germany.

But in spite of Starziczny's less than stellar performance, he was kept on as an agent. His record of achievements may not have been as dazzling as Kempter or Engels, but he still kept the Abwehr informed of British and American activities in South America.

He stayed in Brazil and remained willing and able to keep a sharp eye on the Abwehr's primary objective in South American— British and American ships. Through his contacts, who may have been disgruntled but were still active, he was able to describe to Hamburg the vitally important details needed by U-Boat captains to intercept and identify Allied ships.

Starziczny's reports to Hamburg varied in quality and detail. His better efforts described the cargo, routes, armament, and physical appearance—color of paint used on hull and superstructure, position of funnels and loading cranes, and other items useful to U-Boats—of a variety of British, American, Norwegian, Panamanian, Swedish, and Egyptian vessels.

Starziczny was also able to report that the cruiser HMS *Newcastle* had arrived in Rio de Janeiro in June 1941 and mentioned the departure dates of ore-carrying freighters leaving for the British Isles.

In short, Starziczny did his best. But he was frequently hindered by the clumsiness of his subordinates and by his own carelessness. On one occasion, an uncoded message was sent to Germany through the mail; fortunately for Starziczny, the postal censor did not bother to open the letter. Another time, a contact devised his own code, a "broken English," which was devised to confuse the postal censor or any other unwanted reader. The code was certainly a good one. No one was able to decipher it—including Abwehr cryptanalysts in Hamburg.

Despite everything—the ill will of other agents, shortage of funds, brainless subordinates, and his own lackadaisical attitude— he kept sending his reports in to Hamburg. The way the Abwehr looked at things, even a dim-witted agent had to do something right once in a while.

Starziczny provided Hamburg with moments of comic relief, as well as occasional alarm and aggravation, but any number of other German-born or pro-German agents were also at work in South America. Most of these, like Kempter and Engels, did their job with calculated efficiency, with few mistakes or slip-ups.

The U.S. State Department tried to influence President Vargas to curb German spy activity in Brazil, but Vargas was not willing to cooperate. It was not that he was anti-American, or even anti-British. He just did not want to antagonize Germany by expelling their agents from his country, or even by taking steps to curtail their activities.

Neither the FBI nor MI.5 was in a position to do anything to stop the Abwehr agents. The FBI probably could have sent its own men to Brazil to disrupt Engels, Kempter, and the others. So could have MI.5. But neither organization would have acted without the consent and cooperation of the Vargas regime. And neither organization was willing to risk going against Vargas and violating his "neutrality."

The FBI and MI.5 dealt with the spy situation in South America in different ways. The FBI pretended the German spies were not really all that important to the Abwehr and were not doing much damage to the Allied war effort—even though the agency knew very well that the opposite was true.

But at least the FBI acknowledged that there were enemy spies in South America. MI.5 wouldn't even do this. British counterintelligence pretended that the spies weren't even there. This was their way of justifying their inactivity—there was no use to take action against somebody who doesn't exist.

CHAPTER 8

"You Ought To Be Ashamed of Yourself!"

• • • • •

BECAUSE GEORGE DASCH HAD BEEN RESPONSIBLE FOR THE CAPTURE OF six trained German saboteurs within days of their landing, had convinced Ernest Burger to join him in reporting Operation Pastorius to the U.S. authorities, and was responsible for the foiling of a potentially successful sabotage operation, FBI Director J. Edgar Hoover feared that Dasch might become a heroic figure in the public eye. Even more, he was afraid that the story of Dasch's actions might make the FBI appear inept. Hoover did not intend to let either possibility happen.

George Dasch and Ernest Burger went on trial for sabotage and other lesser charges, including illegal entry into the United States, along with the other six Operation Pastorius defendants. Dasch still insisted upon pleading "not guilty," in spite of J. Edgar Hoover's efforts to persuade him to change his plea.

Dasch's appointed defense council was Colonel Carl Ristine. Col. Ristine said that he would do his best to defend Dasch, but he didn't hold out much hope to his client. He said that it looked like they were backed up to "a stone wall." The chance of acquittal, especially in a military tribunal, was one in a million.

The case against the other six men was fairly simple and straightforward; they had no grounds for their defense. Herbert Haupt and Richard Quirin insisted that they had no intention of performing any sabotage, but had no evidence to support their claim. Edward Kerling also said that he had no enthusiasm for the sabotage operation, and Heinrich Heinck said more or less the same thing. Neither of them could back up their stories, either. Werner Thiel said that he had been trapped into becoming part of Operation

117

Pastorius by Walter Kappe. Hermann Neubauer told the story that he had only been following orders.

These tales of entrapment and only following orders were not very convincing. It did not take much of an effort by the prosecution to make these stories look totally ridiculous and unbelievable.

Dasch and Burger based their defense on the fact that they had gone to the FBI voluntarily, and that their information had been directly responsible for the breakup of the sabotage plot. They had a good deal of evidence to support this argument; J. Edgar Hoover himself could have testified to the fact that Dasch's help had been invaluable. But as it turned out, their defense had no more effect on the court than the testimony of their six fellow defendants.

Before the trial had proceeded very far, Dasch became convinced that it was never supposed to have been a fair trial. For one thing, he had no confidence at all in his defense council and had the feeling that Col. Ristine was under orders not to press his defense too strenuously.

One of the many things that bothered Dasch was the fact that Col. Ristine did not call any of the character witnesses that Dasch had suggested. He had submitted a listing of seven people who had known him before the war and could have testified to the fact that Dasch had taken part in anti-Nazi demonstrations; had served in the U.S. Army; and had a strong affection for the United States. These witnesses would have strengthened the defense; Ristine refused to call any of them as witnesses.

Nor did Col. Ristine call J. Edgar Hoover to ask him about how Dasch and Burger helped the FBI, or about his promise of a presidential pardon for Dasch, to be given in exchange for a "guilty" plea. (Hoover probably would have denied this, anyway, even under oath.)

Another point that disturbed Dasch was the fact that Colonel Ristine did nothing to break down the testimony of Coastguardsman John Cullen, the "beach pounder" who had stumbled across Dasch and the other three from *U-202* on the beach at Amagansett. Cullen's testimony was particularly damaging to the case, but Ristine attempted only a superficial cross-examination. He should have shown that Dasch actually went out of his way to call attention to himself and allowed Cullen to take a good look at him before allowing him to get away. Instead, Ristine only proved that Dasch did not attack Cullen, which had no effect at all on his defense.

118

If Dasch was not happy with Ristine's handling of his case, the prosecution was more than pleased. So was J. Edgar Hoover. When Hoover and Dasch first met, Hoover had promised a "good counsel." Now Dasch realized exactly what he meant. He also realized that the promise of a full presidential pardon within six months had been long forgotten.

George Dasch was not the only one in court who was convinced that his trial was anything but fair. Second Lieutenant John Murdock, the officer in charge of the Montauk Point radar station, was summoned as a witness. His experience at the trial seems to confirm Dasch's suspicions.

At one point during the questioning, Lt. Murdock was asked if he had seen any sign of the German U-Boat on the morning of the landing. When Murdock replied that he had seen nothing, the interrogating officer "got pretty excited." He next asked Lt. Murdock the range of the radar set at Montauk Point—a highly classified subject.

Murdock, a brand new second lieutenant, did not know if he should answer the question or not, since it dealt with top secret information. He asked the president of the court, Major General Frank R. McCoy, for instructions. Gen. McCoy told Murdock to answer the question. (The range was about 150 miles.)

Murdock realized that such highly secret information would not normally be given in front of eight men on trial, especially at that stage of the war. U-Boats were operating off the Atlantic coast, and torpedoing freighters just outside New York harbor. Had there been any chance of either Dasch or Burger being found not guilty, Murdock knew that he would never had been instructed to give such closely guarded information in their presence.

At that point, Murdock knew that none of the accused would be seeing the outside world again. The verdict was already in.

For his own part, Dasch did not do anything to help his case. A highly nervous individual under any circumstances, at the trial he was almost uncontrollable. He shouted, "You ought to be ashamed of yourself!" at Attorney General Biddle several times. His answers on the witness stand rambled and were so badly phrased that they frequently made no sense at all.

When Attorney General Biddle asked why he did not contact the FBI right away, Dasch said that he had three reasons. He only gave two, and only one of these—he was a "mental and nervous wreck"—made any sense. Replies to other questions were even less coherent. Also, he argued angrily with Col. Ristine, "acted up," according to one account, and "created unpleasant situations." J. Edgar Hoover, who was present throughout the trial, could be well satisfied.

Ernest Burger remained calm while on the witness stand; his testimony was clear and straightforward. He gave his reasons for turning against the Nazi regime, even though he had once been a storm trooper, and for undermining Operation Pastorius: he had been falsely arrested by the SS and was bitter over being left in prison by his so-called friends and comrades. Attorney General Biddle seemed satisfied with them.

Burger's testimony also supported Dasch's defense and his contention that he had never intended to go through with Operation Pastorius. Burger confirmed the fact that Dasch was not a Nazi and had thoughts about upsetting the sabotage operation as far back as sabotage school at Quenzsee.

The questions and testimony went on for nearly three weeks; on July 27, 1942, the trial finally came to an end. It had been a good show, if entirely one-sided. The verdict did not surprise anyone.

Because it had been a military trial, the sentences of the eight convicted men was handed down by the president of the United States, who is also commander in chief of the armed forces. All eight men were found guilty on all charges. President Franklin D. Roosevelt sentenced them to death.

But in a move that astonished and angered J. Edgar Hoover, President Roosevelt commuted the sentences of George Dasch and Ernest Burger. He decided that Dasch and Burger should be shown clemency because they had gone to the FBI, regardless of their motives. Burger's sentence was commuted to life imprisonment; Dasch's to 30 years.

So J. Edgar Hoover had not been able to get rid of George Dasch, after all. (He never seemed to be troubled about Burger, probably because he was always so passive.) But he had him in prison, where nobody would hear his story. He would see to that.

As it turned out, the Operation Pastorius saboteurs were neither shot nor hanged. At the district jail in Washington, D.C., electrocution had replaced the hangman's gallows in the 1930s. A separate execution chamber, with a one-way window that allowed witnesses to see into the chamber without being seen, had been built to house the electric chair in 1940.

On the morning of August 8, 1942, the six condemned men had breakfast of scrambled eggs, toast, and bacon. After they had eaten, their heads were shaved by the prison barber, as was the calf of one leg. Then, they were taken to Death Row, in another part of the prison. Death Row is about 100 yards from the execution chamber.

The exact order in which the men were executed was kept secret. But it is a District Jail tradition that multiple executions proceed in alphabetical order, which means that Herbert Haupt went first. "Haupt was seated in the electric chair at one minute past noon," one witness later wrote.

After Haupt was seated in the chair—a plain, unvarnished wooden chair, made in the prison's wood shop—he was strapped in. He was held steady by leather straps around both legs, both arms, his waist, and his jaw. A rubber mask, with openings for the nose and mouth, was then placed over his face. (Somebody circulated the joke that a condemned man had once objected to the mask because it was used at every execution and was therefore unsanitary.)

Next, a metal helmet was placed over Haupt's head; a damp sponge inside the helmet made contact with his shaved skull. A clamp, which also had a dampened sponge inside, was attached to the shaved leg. Electrical cables were then attached to the helmet an clamp.

With Haupt prepared for execution, the chamber was then vacated.

The same procedure was used on each man. After Haupt, it was Heinrich Heinck, then Edward Kerling, Hermann Neubauer, Werner Thiel, and finally Richard Quirin. Each of them entered the chamber in a "stunned, confused, trance-like state." Each execution took an average of ten minutes and thirty seconds. The entire execution, from first to last, lasted one hour and three minutes.

This was considered the fastest multiple execution on record. It required a considerable amount of energy and effort on the part of the executioner.

The body of a man who has just been put to death in the electric chair requires very careful handling. It is usually still smoking from the powerful electric current that surged through it, and the inside of the chamber stinks of burning flesh—the body was literally cooked by electricity. Any buttons or zippers on the dead man's clothing are very hot, hot enough to burn anyone who touches them while handling the body, such as the physician who examines the corpse and pronounces, "This man is dead."

The last man was pronounced dead at 1:04 P.M. The bodies were removed from the prison grounds by ambulances, which were protected from reporters and the curious by soldiers armed with machine guns.

All six men were buried in a weed-covered potters field in Washington called Blue Plains. Their headstones consisted of unpainted slabs of wood. No names were inscribed on the markers, only Numbers 278 through 281.

George Dasch and Ernest Burger were transferred to the federal prison at Danbury, Connecticut, to begin serving their sentences. Dasch was moved to various other prisons during the next few years, including Atlanta and Leavenworth. He was refused permission to have any means of communication with the outside world. Authorities even refused to let him have a pencil, in case he should write out his testimony and somehow smuggle it out of prison.

Others who were linked with Operation Pastorius also went to prison. Hedy Engemann, Edward Kerling's fiancee, served 3 years for treason and lesser charges. Helmut Leiner, Kerling's friend on Long Island, was sentenced to 18 years in prison, but was paroled in 1954.

J. Edgar Hoover got everything he wanted out of the trial of the eight men. He got the recognition he wanted for himself and his bureau and was credited as a national hero for "rounding up" eight enemy saboteurs within days of their landing. President Franklin D. Roosevelt even authorized a bill for an "appropriate medal of honor" for Hoover. His reputation as a "Stork Club detective" had been forgotten, just as he had planned.

Articles in *Reader's Digest* and other magazines repeated Hoover's version of events—that Hoover and his "G-men" were responsible for breaking up the sabotage conspiracy; that George Dasch was only marginally responsible for the demise of Operation Pastorius; and that Dasch had only given himself up to save his own neck, at the expense of the other men. Ernest Burger is usually either left out of these magazine articles, or only mentioned in passing.

Newspaper and magazine accounts went out of their way to praise Hoover and the FBI and vilify Dasch. Some overenthusiastic writers even embellished their stories to make the Germans look inept. For instance, one version insists that Coastguardsman John Cullen, who stumbled across George Dasch in the fog at Amagansett, cleverly induced Dasch to make self-incriminating statements.

The FBI even produced a five-page press release on the incident, called "George John Dasch, and the Nazi Saboteurs." In this circular, the bureau implies that it was their interrogation of Dasch in Washington that led to his giving evidence against the other seven men. "During the next several days," the handout says about Dasch, "he was thoroughly interrogated and he furnished the identities of the other saboteurs, possible locations for some, and data which would enable their more expeditious apprehension." All of this happened after he was "taken into custody."

The reason for Dasch's turning himself in, according to this press release, was that his "resolution to be a saboteur for the Fatherland faltered" after Coastguardsman Cullen found his party on the beach. "Perhaps he thought the whole project so grandiose as to be impractical and wanted to protect himself before some of his companions took action on similar doubts," the press release said. In other words, Dasch only went to the FBI because he wanted to turn his "companions" in before they got the chance to turn him in.

None of the others, including Ernest Burger, ever hinted that they thought the sabotage operation had any chance of failure. Dasch decided to go to the FBI because he thought Operation Pastorius would succeed, and he did not want any sabotage carried out against American facilities. None of the six men who were executed ever went on record as intending to go to U.S. authorities about their sabotage mission. This is just another example of J. Edgar Hoover's attempt to polish his own image at Dasch's expense.

Hoover did such an outstanding job of circulating the "official FBI" version that it endured for years. Twenty five years after World War II ended, an article in *American Heritage* magazine called "The Spies Who Came In from the Sea" retold the Operation Pastorius story. The article virtually ignores the importance of the role played by George Dasch, and Ernest Burger to a lesser degree, in stopping the sabotage operation.

"The spectacle of eight saboteurs sneaking across the Atlantic only to run into the arms of the waiting G-men contained the perfect ingredients for national satisfaction," the article stated matter-of-factly. The "spectacle" was mainly fictional, which the article does not mention.

A footnote discloses that the author "corresponded with FBI Director J. Edgar Hoover."

In Berlin, the news of the operation's quick demise came as an unexpected shock. Col. von Lahousen noted, "Since early morning, we have been receiving radio reports . . . announcing the arrest of all participants in Operation Pastorius."

The response of other high-ranking officers was not as calm and even-tempered. Adm. Dönitz, in command of Germany's U-Boat fleet, was outraged. He and Abwehr chief Adm. Canaris were not the greatest of friends, to begin with. They had known each other before the war and did not get along very well. Dönitz blamed the Abwehr for the failure of Operation Pastorius and is said to have refused any further use of his submarines in any future Abwehr missions. (U-Boats would be used again for similar jobs, however.)

Adolf Hitler was just as angry. He shouted at Canaris and Lahousen for their stupidity and inefficiency. At one point in his tirade, he is reported to have yelled, "Why didn't you use Jews for that?" Canaris and Lahousen only stood in silence, enduring the verbal abuse until they were dismissed.

Colonel von Lahousen passed the blame along to Lieutenant Walter Kappe, who had been in charge of Operation Pastorius. Kappe was given a sharp reprimand, but he explained that the failure of the operation had nothing to do with any laxness or inefficiency on his part. The training of the eight saboteurs had been thorough, he insisted—the explosives they worked with had been the best the Abwehr could supply, and they even had been given demonstrations of how to blow up an aluminum plant by the technical staff of I. G. Farben's aluminum works.

In short, Kappe explained, he was blameless for the operation's untimely demise. His argument was persuasive, as they usually were. Kappe talked his way out of trouble, once again, and stayed on in the Abwehr.

Admiral Wilhelm Canaris and Colonel Erwin von Lahousen could console themselves with the knowledge that Operation Pastorius was only one failure among numerous attempts. There were many other operations against not only the United States, but against Britain as well. Some were sabotage missions, similar to Operation Pastorius;

others involved espionage, spy activities to learn British and American military secrets. Some had already been put into effect. Others were still in the planning stage. They would continue to give J. Edgar Hoover and his British counterpart at MI.5, Sir David Petrie, many frustrating days and nights.

Two footnotes involve J. Edgar Hoover's role in covering up the facts of Operation Pastorius. Both incidents happened after the war had ended.

In the autumn of 1945, staff reporters at *Newsweek* magazine got wind of the real story behind the sabotage operation and of George Dasch's actual role in the affair. *Newsweek* intended to run the story, naming names and telling what Hoover did to Dasch. But Hoover found out that *Newsweek* had the story and tried to keep it from being published.

Although Hoover did not succeed in killing the story outright, he did manage to have it watered down. The *Newsweek* account, which ran in the November 12, 1945, edition, reported that George Dasch and Ernest Burger were responsible for defusing Operation Pastorius, but it did not mention Hoover's repeated efforts to persuade Dasch to plead guilty to charges of sabotage, or the one-sided trial and predetermined verdict. It was written to cover up Hoover's real part in the Pastorius trial. J. Edgar Hoover's name is mentioned exactly twice in the article; both times, it is simply to identify him as the FBI's director.

Even though the story was in one of the country's leading news magazines, it did not make much of a dent in public opinion. Hoover's version of events had been circulating for over three years by that time, and the public had been thoroughly indoctrinated.

Even so, this censored version of the *Newsweek* article brought a response that Hoover probably did not appreciate. In the December 3, 1945, edition of the magazine, this letter, from a U.S. Army sergeant named Frederick L. Anker of Fort Bragg, North Carolina, appeared:

> I have just finished the story of Dasch and Burger. Frankly, I am shocked. Obviously, they not only turned state's evidence but also did not do any harm to this country—nor did they intend to do so. Therefore, it seems to me that these men possibly did more good to the United States than one or two whole United States armies. Instead of keeping them in prison, we should give them houses and land where they could live decently for the rest of their lives.

The second incident took place in 1948, when Dasch and Burger were released on a pardon from President Harry S. Truman. It is customary to pardon enemy spies whenever a war comes to an end. Dasch and Burger were also to be deported to Germany.

As soon as J. Edgar Hoover found out about the pardon, he once again sprang into action. At his insistence, the two men were rushed out of the country. Dasch was whisked away so quickly that neither his American-born wife, who had spent most of the war interned in Bermuda, nor his attorney knew anything about the pardon or the deporting. They didn't find out until he was already on his way back to Germany.

Probably recalling the *Newsweek* article, Hoover intended that Dasch be kept from telling his story to the press.

CHAPTER 9

Spy Nests and Clandestine Operations

• • • • •

FBI DIRECTOR J. EDGAR HOOVER CONCLUDED THAT "THE BEST WAY TO control Nazi espionage in the United States was to wipe out the spy nests in Latin America." Hoover was certainly not having much success in wiping out German spy organizations inside the United States. Abwehr agents continued to send intelligence reports to Germany, frequently via Albrecht Engels and Friedrich Kempter in Brazil. And, apart from making private remarks about spy nests, he wasn't doing very much about Latin American agents, either.

Brazil wasn't the only Latin American country that harbored German agents. The Abwehr had 40 agents in Mexico, who were organized into three separate networks. They were very well organized and sent information on military, industrial, and commercial activities in the United States to Abwehr sections in Hamburg and Berlin, as well as in Cologne.

The Abwehr also had at least one agent, and probably more, in Cuba. Cuban dictator Fulgencia Batista was not inclined to interfere with spy activities, and many pro-Fascist Cubans would gladly have gone to the assistance of Nazi Germany. But at least one man was known to have been active.

The agent in question was Heinz August Luning, who went by the name Enrique August Luni. Luning was born in Hamburg in 1910. During the 1930s, he traveled extensively throughout the Caribbean as a sightseer. The knowledge of Spanish he had acquired in his travels, as well as his knowledge of the Caribbean, made him of prime interest to Adm. Canaris and his organization. In 1940, he joined the Abwehr.

Luning was thoroughly trained for his job as a spy. He was taught the skills of the espionage trade—radio operation and making secret inks, in Bremen; special courses in Cuban Spanish and geography of the Central Atlantic area, in Madrid; and memorized codes and contact addresses, in Barcelona.

On September 30,1941, Luning arrived in Havana aboard the Spanish liner *Ciudad de Madrid*. Under the name Enrique Luni, he invested in a dress shop and dressmaking business, as a cover for his espionage activities. He also built a powerful radio transmitter and spent a good deal of his time near the waterfront. Luning's favorite hangout was a cafe at Porto Chico. From the cafe, which offered an excellent view of Havana harbor, he could see every ship that came and departed.

Most of Luning's reports to the Abwehr were sent via letter. Every day, he sent a letter to a contact in Madrid or Barcelona; these letters were sent to an innocent-looking business address, which was also a cover. Each of these notes was signed by a different name—in case they were opened, daily letters sent by the same person might arouse suspicion. When a bit of news or information was of particular urgency, Luning sent it by radio.

These reports were sent out every day for 11 months. They had to clear British censors in Bermuda before being sent on to Spain and, from there, to Germany. The British censors duly passed them on to their destination.

Eventually, the number of letters began to attract interest. Alert censors in Bermuda noticed that all the letters to the Madrid and Barcelona addresses were sent by the same person; even though they all had different signatures, all the notes were in the same handwriting. Photostats were made of each letter. Then the letters were put back in their envelopes and sent on their way.

When the Bermuda censors had collected enough photostats, they notified the FBI branch in Havana. Federal agents kept Luning under surveillance. When they were satisfied that Luning was involved in espionage, they notified the Havana police. Luning was arrested on August 15,1942.

A Cuban military trial found Luning guilty of espionage, and sentenced him to death. This produced an outcry from pro-Nazi sympathizers, and pressure was brought to bear to reduce Luning's sentence. But the sentence was carried out—Luning was shot by a firing squad on November 8, 1942.

Luning was tracked down and caught, but many others were not. Another spy working for the Nazi cause, Richard Dotres, simply vanished from sight after the American investigators were tipped off concerning his activities. Dotres had been in Havana from March 1941 until the autumn of 1942, apparently doing what Luning was doing, but Dotres got away with it.

Another base for German intelligence, far more active than either Mexico or Cuba, was Argentina. The main operator in Argentina was Johannes Siegfried Becker. Becker was not an employee of the Abwehr, but an officer in the SD, the security branch of Heinrich Himmler's SS. He had spent three years in Argentina, from 1937 to 1940, when he was recalled to Germany. But he was sent back to Buenos Aries in 1942, assigned to reorganize and direct spy activities in Argentina.

Becker organized the spy network into three sections: his own, the "red" group; the embassy, "blue" group; and the "green" group, which collected information on American municipal and industrial activities. Most of this data was obtained from U.S. newspapers, technical magazines, and monitored radio broadcasts—the luxuries of a free society used against itself.

Also helpful were observations of the Argentine diplomatic staff, who tried to intercept classified embassy documents and eavesdropped on private conversations, and the advice of Argentine military officers who had been trained in the United States.

The government of Argentina was unashamedly pro-Axis. Officials not only encouraged Becker and his subagents, but also did all they could to help them. Juan Peron, one of the leaders of the ruling military junta, was on friendly terms with the head of Becker's "green" section, an attorney named Johann Leo Harnishch. Argentina's foreign minister referred to Americans as "Yankee bastards" and promised to keep Becker and his agents supplied with as much information as possible because "the destiny of Argentina" depended upon Germany winning the war.

Although the United States brought economic pressure to bear against the Argentine government, Becker's activities continued, the same as before. Reports to Germany consisted mainly of trade information between Argentina and the Allies—grain and livestock bought by Britain, raw materials shipped to the United States.

When these actions had no effect, the United States decided to take more direct measures. First, there was a return to "gunboat diplomacy"—warships were sent to "visit" neighboring Uruguay. Also, there were threats to freeze Argentine assets in the United States. But Becker kept on sending his reports to Germany, with government protection.

Getting his information became a bit more difficult—American newspapers and magazines were harder to come by because of restrictions imposed by the United States. But Becker still managed to get the information he needed and kept sending his reports across to Germany. Besides radio broadcasts, Becker also sent information via sailors on Spanish vessels who passed the reports along to Germany after reaching port. By this time, it was no longer safe to send anything by air mail—there was too great a risk of messages being intercepted.

Becker kept sending his reports to Germany right to the end of the war. He finally stopped in 1945, when Germany had no further need for the material he was sending.

Neither the FBI nor MI.5 was doing anything to stop the South American spy networks. But beginning in 1941, British Intelligence began intercepting Abwehr radio transmissions to and from Brazil. Naval Intelligence in London picked up the signals. A deciphering center at Bletchley Park, in Buckinghamshire, transformed the code in to clear text. Through these intercepts, MI.5 was kept advised of German knowledge of British and American shipping activities. Intelligence also learned about the secret courier service that carried the information out of Brazil, Argentina, and other South American countries and sent it to Germany.

All of this was done in the strictest secrecy. Not even British agents stationed in South America were told about these monitoring activities.

The Americans were also intercepting and deciphering messages from Latin America. Not just from Brazil and Argentina, but also messages between Mexico and Germany. The primary deciphering center was in Texas, but more than 30 substations were set up at army outposts in various locations.

These interceptions did not do anything to stem shipping losses, for all the brave efforts. Counterintelligence in both Britain and the United States may have known more about the German monitoring of ship movements, but losses to U-Boats kept increasing throughout 1941 and 1942.

In December 1941, the United States was drawn into the war. Japanese carrier-based aircraft attacked the U.S. Pacific Fleet at Pearl Harbor, Hawaii, on December 7. Four days later, Germany declared war on the United States. The situation in South America, and for German agents in South American countries, began to change.

The United States brought pressure to bear on Brazilian President Getulio Vargas—if he severed all Axis ties, he was assured that immediate additional military and economic assistance would be extended. But along with this assurance, Vargas received a threat. It was implied, but not stated outright, that if Brazil did not comply with American requests, an economic boycott would be imposed.

Vargas got the message. He was convinced that his better interests were with the Allies and was prepared to back up his new convictions. On January 28, 1942, the Brazilian foreign minister announced that his government was breaking relations with Berlin, Tokyo, and Rome.

Brazilian police were told to intensify surveillance of Axis nationals. Travel for Axis citizens was also restricted, and licenses to own firearms and explosives were revoked. President Vargas issued a ban on the sending of all coded radio transmissions.

This was a step in the right direction, at least as far as the British and Americans were concerned, but even these measures were not very effective in stopping German agents. The radio ban, for instance, only affected reports on airplanes and airfields. The radio sets were still in the hands of the Abwehr employees, anyway.

The networks run by Kempter and Engels, as well as by other Axis nationals, continued to function. Kempter kept sending his intelligence to Germany, mostly shipping movements and sightings of British and American warships. The Engels group also sent a regular stream of information on Allied shipping and naval activities.

Shortly after the United States entered the war, the British liner *Queen Mary* stopped over at Rio de Janeiro on her way to Australia. The *Queen Mary* was traveling without escort and was loaded with American troops. An Italian agent sent word to Rome when the *Queen Mary* departed Rio; the signal was passed along to U-Boat

Command. But the ship was able to evade any waiting U-Boats and docked safely in Australia. The incident caused more than a few anxious moments for both the British and Americans, who had intercepted and decoded the Italian's radio message. Other ships did not have the speed to outrun U-Boats that the *Queen Mary* had and were not as lucky.

Probably the most damaging development for Axis agents in Brazil was the merging of British and American intelligence operations. It was also the most surprising development—to the British and Americans, as well as to the Abwehr. The U.S. government even allowed the British to establish a "clandestine operations" center in New York. President Roosevelt wanted "the closest possible marriage between the FBI and British Intelligence," and managed to keep this unorthodox arrangement a secret, even from the State Department.

Because of Anglo-American cooperation, and also because the Brazilian government was no longer "neutral"—that is, it no longer chose to look the other way—both Engels and Kempter began to encounter increasing difficulties from the police and government officials. Agents were arrested, radio transmitters were confiscated, and the harassment of Axis nationals by the police increased.

British counterintelligence was also lending a hand, or at least doing its best, to deactivate the Abwehr network. Imperial Censorship, which operated from the Princess Hotel in Bermuda, was set up to intercept all postal, radio, and telegraph communications. Imperial Censorship was very efficient at its job, but its excellent work was sometimes wasted when officials at MI.5 and other branches of British Intelligence either ignored the advice or acted too late to take advantage of it.

In the basement of the Princess Hotel, a luxurious pink colonial building, British technicians opened letters, read and photographed the contents, and resealed the envelopes in such a way that no one could tell that they had ever been tampered with. They could even remove a diplomatic seal and replace it so perfectly that not even chemical or ultraviolet tests would reveal anything amiss.

But before these expert methods could be put to use, a letter would have to be intercepted and opened. Both Engels and Kempter, as well as the hapless Starziczny and possibly scores of other Axis agents, sent literally hundreds of air mail letters that reached Germany undetected.

The use of microdots did not make Imperial Censorship's job any easier. A report on a convoy sailing, giving time of sailing, destination, number of ships, and even the composition of escorting naval ships, could be sent in plain language without fear of detection. The message would simply be disguised as a period at the end of a sentence, glued onto to the face of a perfectly harmless and meaningless personal letter.

The staff at the Princess Hotel—it was discovered that tall, leggy females were the most skilled at this type of work—could examine 2,000 pieces of mail for suspicious contents during the stopover time of an air mail clipper. The number of messages that reached Hamburg and Berlin, however, indicates that most of the Abwehr messages did not go by way of Bermuda, or that the Imperial Censorship girls were not as good at their jobs as their reputation.

British agents in South America took a much more direct method in trying to stop German Intelligence agents. They tried to murder Friedrich Kempter on more than one occasion. One attempt was made in January 1942. Kempter was sitting at home, reading a magazine, when he heard a gunshot. The bullet passed through the open window of Kempter's sitting room and struck the wall close by his head. This attempt did not intimidate Kempter, however. He kept on sending, the same as before.

The FBI managed to learn the identity of Kempter, Engels, and other agents in Brazil. This was mainly due to the carelessness and complacency of the agents themselves—they made the mistake of sending their real names on some reports, instead of their code names. The inactivity of British and American counterintelligence actually did have some positive results, after all. By March 1942, the FBI and MI.5 knew the names and addresses of every Abwehr agent operating in Brazil.

But knowing the agents' identities was one thing. Shutting down their spy networks was another matter entirely. The Brazilian organizations continued to inform the Abwehr and U-Boat Command of Allied shipping. During the early months of 1942, the Allies were losing a ship nearly every day to German submarines. Other information, unrelated to the convoys, also continued to reach German Intelligence.

Time was running out for the Abwehr's men in Brazil, though. Circumstance, which had once favored the German spies, had turned against them. The Brazilian authorities, Anglo-American cooperation, and especially the faltering military fortunes of the Third Reich, finally combined to destroy a first-rate espionage organization.

Albrecht Engels and Friedrich Kempter both were arrested in March 1942, on the same day. Their contacts and subagents were also rounded up during the next few days. Some of them managed to take their radios and leave Brazil. Most escaped either to Argentina or Chile, both of which remained actively pro-Axis, where they continued to send messages to Germany.

Albrecht Engels was sentenced to 30 years in prison for espionage; Friedrich Kempter was given 25 years. Even after the war, Engels was still not fully trusted by Brazilian authorities. The newspaper *Jornal do Brasil* of February, 1978, mentioned that Engels' name was on the list of 13,000 "potentially troublesome individuals" that had been drawn up by the Ministry of Justice. This was prior to U.S. President Jimmy Carter's impending visit to Brazil later that year.

Josef Starziczny, the Abwehr employee who got his information in a twist as often as not, was also arrested for espionage. Like Albrecht Engels, Starziczny was sentenced to 30 years in prison, the maximum sentence. Apparently, incompetence was not considered an extenuating circumstance by the Brazilian magistrate.

For over two years, the Abwehr was given a steady input of information, some of it vital, by its Brazilian contacts. Most of these agents were steady and dependable, supplying data on shipping and other items that was unfailingly accurate. The fact that this highly useful network was eventually dismantled was not the fault of the agents themselves. If President Vargas had chosen to resist American economic pressure, as the regimes of Argentina and Chile had done, Kempter, Engels, and the others could have stayed right where they were.

Without American pressure, the German agents never would have been flushed out—their demise was the result of President Vargas' eventual cooperation with the Allies, not the efforts of either the FBI or MI.5. And had the German military efforts not begun to fail—in North Africa and in Russia, the once-invincible Wehrmacht had been stopped and was being decimated—President Vargas might have gone on hemming and hawing with the Americans, instead of cracking down on the German agents. He could have very easily kept on his talk about "neutrality," promising to take action against the Abwehr network, while actually continuing to look the other way.

The end of Engels' and Kempter's networks, and even Starziczny's, came as a great relief to the Allies. It was a serious blow to the Abwehr, as well as to Adm. Dönitz and the captains of the Atlantic U-Boat fleet.

Presumably as a gesture of good will toward the Americans, President Vargas became an active belligerent against Germany after he drove out the Abwehr's spies. He fired pro-Nazi members of his government, including the head of the Brazilian police, and replaced them with men who favored the Allied cause.

Vargas also permitted the Brazilian Air Force to participate in joint patrols with American airplanes. Joint U.S./Brazilian air patrols began operating together out of the strategic northeastern air bases, which had been the objects of interest to Albrecht Engels two years before. In the spring of 1942, they accounted for several U-Boats sunk.

After Vargas had allowed German spies to roam at will in his country, the Nazi regime was both puzzled and angered by his sudden change of sides. Berlin was not happy about this turn of events, to put it mildly. In retaliation for the attacks on its U-Boats, the German navy sent ten submarines into Brazilian waters. In July 1942, these U-Boats sank three Brazilian ships in five days.

Now it was Brazil's turn to be outraged. Crowds throughout Brazil demonstrated against Germany in noisy street rallies. On August 22, bowing to pressure from within Brazil, President Vargas declared war on both Germany and Italy. The German espionage network, which had played hell with both the Americans and British, was now officially outlawed.

FBI Director J. Edgar Hoover took responsibility for closing down the Axis espionage networks, although the FBI's role was, at best, incidental.

A "Special Intelligence Service" had been set up to "wipe out the spy nests in Latin America," as Hoover put it. This SIS was a combined effort between Hoover, Assistant Secretary of State Adolf Berle, Army Intelligence (G-2), and Naval Intelligence. It was to be an extension of the FBI, to combat "financial, economic, political, and subversive activities detrimental to the security of the United States."

A special SIS training school was also approved by President Roosevelt. But the SIS program did not have very many Spanish and Portuguese-speaking applicants, which made the training schedule longer and more difficult.

The school curriculum had to start from scratch—teaching Latin American history and customs, as well as languages. And not all of the students were able to pick up the languages as quickly as it had been hoped, which resulted in further delays before they could be sent to South America.

The FBI/SIS did have some minor successes, such as discovering the identity of Kempter, Engels, and Starziczny. But they never stopped the sending of any reports. And they never came close to justifying the FBI claim for "the break-up of the Brazilian ring," which did not take place until Brazil and Germany severed relations.

J. Edgar Hoover would have benefited by copying MI.5's discreet silence concerning the success of German spies in South America, and its own lack of success in putting an end to this espionage network. But discreet silence was never one of Hoover's virtues.

CHAPTER 10

Internal Matters

• • • • •

ONE OF THE MOST SHADOWY AND MYSTERIOUS OF GERMAN AGENTS, IN either Britain or the United States, was a Welshman named Gwyn Evans. Evans was not an employee of the Abwehr. As a matter of fact, he was sent to England to check on Abwehr agents, and to find out why some of them had been caught in recent months—was it because of bad luck, or treachery?

He never did find the answer. But he was able to send back military information from England, much of it closely guarded by strict security, and to keep MI.5 off balance for three frustrating years. This is another episode that Military Intelligence preferred to ignore.

Evans parachuted into Wales from a Luftwaffe aircraft on the night of May 10, 1941, the same night that Rudolph Hess made his mad flight to Scotland. His contact in Wales was Arthur Owen. Unknown to MI.5, Owen was a triple-agent. Counterintelligence officers knew that he was an Abwehr employee and were satisfied that they had "turned" him; his MI.5 code name was "Snow." Besides sending the false data fed to him by MI.5, he also sent genuine information to Berlin—which counterintelligence knew nothing about.

Owen's reports were not to the Abwehr, however; they went out to the SS State Security organization, which had been formed by Heinrich Himmler. Gwen Evans' reports would also be for the SS, instead of Canaris and his staff.

But working for the SS was not the only thing that Evans and Owen had in common. They were also Welsh Nationalists, although Evans was much more ardent than Owen. The Welsh Nats cause was an independent Welsh state, and freedom from what they considered "English rule." Many of the nationalists believed that Adolf Hitler would grant Wales independence if Germany won the war—Owen and Evans were two such believers.

Besides being a Welsh Nationalist, Evans was also half German by birth. His mother was the former Hedwig von Forbath, a loyal German and a Nazi; she never quite got over the fact that Germany lost the Great War. She met Caradog Evans in 1913, while on holiday in Argentina. Caradog Evans was a fervently patriotic Welshman. He was fluent in the Welsh language and had no use for foreigners in general and for the English in particular.

The two were married during World War I; their son Gwyn was born in 1916. Young Gwyn grew up in Argentina, where he learned Welsh from his father and to hate the English from both parents. He was an ethnic Welshman, an Argentinean Welshman—and became more Welsh than the Welsh, the way some Irish-Americans, who have never set eyes on Ireland, become more Irish than the Blarney Stone.

In 1936, Gwyn's parents split up. He went to Germany with his mother. While he was still in Argentina, he had joined the Nazi party, much to his mother's delight. Now, he decided that he would fight against England in the event of war—both for the Glory of the Fatherland, which his mother had drilled into him, and for Free Wales.

After war broke out, Evans was sent off to an espionage training camp in East Prussia. He finished his course and parachuted into Britain in 1941. There, he met any number of seedy and disreputable characters. First and foremost was his contact, Arthur Owen, who was drunk more often than sober. Evans did not trust him; he thought Owen would sell him, or anyone else, out for a free drink.

There was also Paul von Fidrmuc, a Sudeten German who headed a spy network and sent regular reports to Adm. Canaris. But Canaris never found out that all of von Fidrmuc's information was totally useless, since every spy in his "network" was completely fictitious. He received his data from newspapers, magazines, gossip, and reference books, and turned them into authentic-sounding intelligence reports. When contacting the Abwehr, he credited the various bits of data as having come from agents in the field—agents which existed only in his own mind. The Abwehr sent regular payments to von Fidrmuc's spy ring. Von Fidrmuc, of course, kept the payments himself.

Evans also made the acquaintance of Tommy Harris, a wealthy Spanish-speaking art dealer who was also a member of MI-5's "Double-Cross Committee"—the organization that "turned" captured German agents into double-agents working for counterintelligence. Harris was also a homosexual, and a friend of H. A. R. "Kim" Philby.

Philby was also in British Intelligence. His job was to act as liaison between MI.5, which was concerned with espionage inside Britain, and MI.6, which handled spy duties outside the British Isles. No one had any suspicions about Philby's loyalties, which went deeper than either money or nationalism. Gwyn Evans had no idea how Philby and his loyalties were to affect his own life.

Evans' knowledge of music helped him to land a job organizing shows for the troops—he was a trained vocalist and an accomplished choral performer. He was attached to a string quartet made up of four refugees from Holland and was given the task of "popularizing" their repertoire for the forces—playing selections from Gilbert and Sullivan instead of Beethoven. The concerts were not a roaring success, for either the string quartet or their audience. But Evans acquired a good deal of classified information, mainly from the troops his string quartet was supposed to be entertaining.

The troops were Canadians who had never heard of the Official Secrets Act and wouldn't have cared if they had. They made no secret of the fact that they were about to make a landing on the French coast, at Dieppe.

Evans kept his ears open, and sent full details of the impending landings to Germany. At first, he got the Operation's code name wrong, as well as the date that the landings were scheduled to take place, but this was not his fault. The code name was changed from "Operation Rutter" to "Operation Jubilee" for security reasons, and the date was changed because of bad weather.

But he learned enough to warn the German High Command. When Allied forces landed at Dieppe on August 19, 1942—mostly Canadians, with a few British Commandos and American Rangers—the Wehrmacht was alert and waiting. Almost half the force was killed, captured, or wounded. Operation Jubilee was a disaster. If the German forces had not been tipped off in advance, the Allied landing force would never have been so badly mauled.

British Intelligence, and especially the "Double-Cross Committee," were both angry and amazed over the breach of security. They were determined to find the German agent who discovered the facts of Operation Jubilee; when they found him, they would "turn" him into a double-agent, the way they had done with many others.

MI.5 had a suspicion that a German agent was on the loose even before Dieppe. The plane that had dropped Evans over Wales had been spotted, and the burnt remains of a parachute had been discovered in the same area. Counterintelligence even had an idea that the man they wanted was neither German nor English. A captured female spy gave a hint that the man spoke a strange-sounding language but, not knowing Welsh, she could not identify it.

The Russians were as angry as the British over the failure of the Dieppe raid. Ever since Hitler invaded Russia in June 1941, Stalin had been demanding a second front. He wanted an operation in the West to draw some of the forces out of Russia. Dieppe had been that operation, and it ended in disaster.

Soviet Intelligence also discovered that the Germans had been warned in advance of the raid. They suspected that the operation had been deliberately sabotaged by the Allies, to convince the Russians that a full-scale invasion of France would be impossible.

But the KGB's contact in London convinced his superiors that it had been a German agent who warned the enemy, and not an Anglo-American trick. Moscow allowed itself to believe its man in London, and instructed him to find out who and where the mysterious agent was. The man they instructed was Philby—an acquaintance of Evans and a member of the "Double-Cross Committee."

Evans now had the Russians looking for him, in addition to MI.5. But besides learning that their man was probably not German, neither Philby nor his colleagues at counterintelligence had very much to go on. Evans was still at large and still very active.

In 1942, Evans discovered that General Dwight D. Eisenhower would be presented to King George and Queen Elizabeth in a reception at Windsor Castle. Other agents in Britain also discovered that Eisenhower had arrived, but most reported that he would be meeting Their Majesties at Buckingham Palace. Evans also learned that Eisenhower would be commanding an Allied amphibious operation sometime in the near future.

Evans had not done much in the way of spying on Abwehr

agents, which is what he had been sent to Britain for in the first place. But he was having such success in finding top secret information that none of his superiors in Germany had any objections.

At about the same time that he found out about Eisenhower's arrival in England, Evans also learned that the Allies were preparing a full-scale amphibious landing—probably the same one that Eisenhower would be commanding. He did not know where the landing would take place, but he had heard it referred to as Operation "Flama" by Spanish-speaking contacts of Tommy Harris. (Having lived in Argentina for years, Evans spoke Spanish fluently.)

Operation "Flama," or Flame, was actually Operation Torch, the invasion of North Africa, which took place in November 1942. Its Commander was General Dwight D. Eisenhower.

British counterintelligence deciphered a German radio signal which mentioned "Operation Flamme." They realized that it referred to Torch. If they had been amazed by the enemy's knowledge of the Dieppe raid, they were now thoroughly alarmed. MI.5 was now more determined than ever to find out who was sending this damaging information. The Russians were just as determined.

Sometime in 1943, Kim Philby discovered that Paul von Fidrmuc was an Abwehr agent. He also discovered that von Fidrmuc's spy network existed only in his own head. Philby confronted him and made a proposition—if von Fidrmuc revealed how the Germans managed to find out about Operation "Flama," he would keep quiet about his Abwehr connections. He would also make sure that none of his superiors in Germany found out that von Fidrmuc's spy ring was fake, which would allow his profitable little set up to go on.

Von Fidrmuc told Philby all he wanted to know about the mysterious Evans. A short while later, the Abwehr was taken over by the SS, and Adm. Canaris was arrested.

Philby had failed to mention to von Fidrmuc the fact that the Evans story was not for British Intelligence. He wanted the information for his KGB superiors in Moscow.

Although Philby now knew who Evans was, and MI.5 was still trying to find out, nobody knew *where* he was. Evans was still as active as ever. He was also still running musical shows for soldiers and airmen, which gave him an excellent excuse to visit army bases and airfields throughout Britain. Especially in southern England, where the British and Americans were building up their forces for the invasion of German-occupied France—the highly anticipated D-Day landings, code-named "Operation Overlord."

The landings were anticipated by military leaders on both sides of the English Channel. The German High Command knew that the Allies were going to land an amphibious force somewhere along the northern coast of France—it was impossible to hide a military build-up as large as the force being assembled in the south of England. The German generals wanted to know two vital facts: where and when? When would the invasion take place, and on what part of the French coast?

There were many, including Adolf Hitler himself, who thought that the Calais area would be the invasion site, since it was closest to England. But others disagreed; these people held the opinion that the invasion would take place on the Normandy beaches. Evans was among those who thought Normandy would be the place.

His opinion was based solidly upon what he had observed in England. Evans used his job as entertainment organizer to tour the southern coast of England. His pass, thoughtfully provided by British authorities in London, allowed him to pass through military police barricades. Once inside the restricted area, he roamed at will.

He saw military vehicles on every road; supplies being unloaded all along the coast; Portsmouth harbor packed with ships of every description. And he saw troops everywhere: armor, infantry, para-troops.

When he returned to London, Evans sent a long report to Germany. In the report, he told about what he had seen on the south coast; identified many of the units he had seen by division, and sometimes by regiment; and concluded by giving his opinion that Normandy would be the destination of all these troops and their equipment.

His contact in Germany did not seem very impressed, either by Evans' report or his opinion. He asked Evans to make a similar scouting trip into southeastern England especially, and to make a full report of his observations when he returned to London.

The SS sent Evans to Kent and Sussex to find out about the First United States Army Group (FUSAG). Actually, FUSAG was nothing more than an elaborate ruse, a trick to make the Wehrmacht believe that the Allied buildup in southwest England was only a diversion. But intelligence sources in Germany and occupied France kept hearing a lot about this large Army Group. According to the stories, which were being circulated by both British and American Intelligence, the buildup along the Channel coast, and subsequent invasion of Normandy, were only a front, a false invasion staged to draw German troops away from the Calais area. Then, FUSAG would move, launching the *real* invasion near Calais.

After a tour of the southeast of England, Evans became certain of what he had suspected all along—FUSAG did not exist. There were no divisions being held in reserve. There was to be no invasion in the Pas de Calais.

Evans saw a few training bases, but nothing like the masses of men, machinery, vehicles, and equipment he had observed all along the south coast. There was certainly no invasion force in Kent, and nothing resembling any FUSAG. He was now totally convinced that the Allied invasion would be in Normandy. He still did not know exactly when, but at least he had found out where the landings would take place.

Evans returned to London, and sent another report to Germany—FUSAG was a fake. But the decision makers of the German High Command chose not to believe him. They still held that the "real" invasion would be in the Calais vicinity.

Even after the Invasion had actually taken place, on Tuesday, June 6, 1944, the High Command was still holding back forces from Normandy. Evans sent several signals to Germany, repeating that there was no such unit as FUSAG and that the "real" invasion had already taken place at Normandy.

But the High Command refused to listen. They had already made up their minds and did not want to be confused by the facts. Reinforcements, which might have swung the balance to the German army's favor if they had been sent to Normandy, were held in reserve near Calais until it was too late.

Evans had done his job. He found out the exact place that the Allies had chosen for the long-awaited invasion and reported his findings to Germany, but nobody took any notice.

When Evans finally discovered what was going on, that the information being sent out by the British and Americans was being taken as truth while his own reports were ignored, his morale hit rock bottom. He was already disheartened by the death of his mother, who had died in a British air raid on Bremen. He now realized that Germany had no chance of winning the war, and that Adolf Hitler would never be able to free Wales from England.

Disheartened, Evans disappeared from the air waves. He broadcast a final message to Germany, announcing that he would be going away for a week's rest, and left London. Taking his radio with him, he set out for Wales, where he hoped to contact Arthur Owen. Owen had contacts of his own in Germany. If he could be found, maybe he would be able to get a message through for Evans. Maybe Owen could get a report to somebody in the SS or the High Command, to warn about FUSAG and the phony Calais information.

Evans expected to learn that Owen was either drunk or in jail, or both. To his surprise, he was able to locate Owen with almost no difficulty. But Owen was not able to contact anybody in Germany, at least not anybody who would be useful to Evans. Instead, he contacted Philby.

Philby came to Wales as soon as he got Owen's message, and saw Evans in an arranged meeting. Whatever pro-Soviet line he handed Evans, it must have been very persuasive—he recruited the Welsh nationalist into the service of the Soviet Union. Gwyn Evans became an agent of the KGB. Apparently, Philby convinced him that the best way to strike at England was through Russian Intelligence.

At any rate, MI.5 didn't have him, and never did find out his whereabouts or his true identity.

For over three years, Gwyn Evans roamed Britain as he pleased. He even had a security pass, issued by officials in London, which allowed him to enter restricted areas. His detailed reports to Germany, probably several hundred over this period, were based on what he had seen and heard while organizing musical entertainment for British and Allied troops. MI.5 couldn't find him, much less prevent his defection to the Soviet Union.

The information he radioed to Germany did considerable damage to the Allied war effort. Evans told the German High Command about the Dieppe raid, allowing the Wehrmacht to lie in wait for the landing and inflict murderous casualties on the invading troops. He very nearly did the same thing for the D-Day landings, as well. It wasn't his fault that his information was ignored. His messages certainly got through—in spite of British Intelligence's protests that no enemy agent ever operated from British soil.

German sympathizers of Irish nationality, especially members of the Irish Republican Army, presented MI.5 with still more headaches. Irish nationals committed any number of acts of espionage and sabotage against Britain, but MI.5 had an excuse for not doing anything to stop these activities, or at least a partial excuse—many of these incidents were carried out from neutral Ireland.

An American news report claimed that "neutral Ireland was a source of information for the Axis." The Irish government in Dublin disagreed strenuously, protesting that the country was neutral and did not side either with the Allies or the Axis.

But the Irish protest did not have much foundation; the country was used as a base for espionage throughout the war. The German Legation in Dublin was directly responsible for many acts of mischief against the Allies. Germany's minister to Ireland, Eduard Hempel, did his share to help torpedo—sometimes literally—the Allied war effort from his Dublin office.

Shortly after the war began, Hempel radioed Berlin that an American passenger ship, the SS *Iroquis*, would be leaving Ireland for the United States, giving time of departure. He made similar reports regarding other American ships.

As a result of Hempel's report, the German navy was able to find and sink the *Iroquis*. Admiral Erich Raeder said that the information had come from a leak in the American naval attaché's office in Ireland. But the U.S. Navy had no attaché in Ireland.

The German Legation in Dublin resembled a fortress more than an embassy. An armed man always slept on the premises, and three German diplomats and one civil servant carried firearms inside the legation. A particularly nasty guard dog was kept on duty, and all the windows were bolted shut.

The Irish authorities did their best to cut back on Hempel's communications to Berlin, but never attempted to have Hempel recalled to Germany or to have the legation closed. Among the more harmless-sounding items that Hempel sent along to Berlin were weather reports. These reports proved to be of enormous help on at least one occasion.

In 1942, the German warships *Scharnhorst*, *Prinz Eugen*, and *Gneisnau* escaped the British naval blockade and sailed from Brest to Germany through the English Channel. It was a humiliating incident for Britain, having an enemy fleet steam right through the Straits of Dover in broad daylight. The Germans were helped by the fact that their escape was made under cover of rain and heavy clouds, which prevented the ships from being sighted until they were right in the Channel. British sources claimed that the German Navy had acted on weather reports sent from Dublin; the day and time of sailing had been based upon these reports.

Hempel also kept a constant correspondence with Berlin on military matters, information picked up through diplomatic channels. He reported that the *Queen Elizabeth* and *Queen Mary* had been converted into fast troop transports, and that the two liners did not sail in convoys, relying upon their speed to outrun any U-Boats. Also, he told Berlin that airfields in Northern Ireland were being used by the U.S. Army Air Force to keep replacement aircraft and crews, so that they could be rushed to front-line air bases in England when needed.

Of course, he got some things wrong. Hempel once reported that the *Queen Mary* had been sunk off Belfast, with 16,000 American and Canadian troops on board. Berlin soon found out that the *Queen Mary* was still very much afloat and busily carrying troops across the Atlantic. Hempel also overestimated the number of U.S. troops stationed in the North; apparently, he had fears that American troops might be used to intimidate "neutral" Ireland into joining the Allies.

But he kept a sharp eye out for useful news and information, and a suspicious eye for anyone offering information—Hempel was always wary of a British plant in his small but efficient network.

Minister Hempel had reason to be suspicious. He was always receiving offers of assistance from volunteer "spies." Among the volunteers were: a violently anti-English Scottish nationalist; a follower of the English fascist Oswald Mosely; several Irishmen who claimed to be members of the IRA; a German expatriate; and an American engineer with "valuable information" to sell. Most of these turned out to be either crackpots, malcontents, or both. The American was just greedy. He was more interested in collecting 25,000 pounds for his "valuable information" than in spying for Germany.

That was getting to be more and more of a problem for German agents in Ireland—everybody in the country seemed more interested in other things than working for Germany. The Irish Republican Army was especially guilty of letting down the German cause—at least Berlin thought so. After a gaudy beginning—blowing up Hammersmith Bridge and planting bombs in London—the IRA's main activities consisted of squabbling among themselves and demanding more and more money and weapons from Berlin.

The IRA had actually been outlawed in June 1939. Although President Eamon de Valera had been in the IRA himself, he now wanted to settle Ireland's differences with England by peaceful methods, instead of by guerrilla warfare and terrorism.

This did not stop members of the "New" IRA, of course; they carried on with their bomb attacks in Northern Ireland, in England, and in the Republic of Ireland. Members were harried by the police and arrested, but the organization was too firmly rooted to be broken up by the government in Dublin.

The IRA leaders wanted weapons and explosives from the Germans to carry out their own violent campaigns, not just so they could help Germany's military efforts. They did not intend to attack England exclusively; in fact, England was far down on their list of priorities. Members much preferred carrying out attacks in Northern Ireland, as well as against "disloyal" fellow members and rival factions in the republic.

Berlin was becoming increasingly dissatisfied with its friends and, as the war went on, the IRA became less and less cooperative with the Germans. The more money and weapons sent to the Irish, at risk to valuable U-Boats and their crews, the less the IRA seemed willing to do in return. Submarines made frequent deliveries of arms and explosives, but the Irish never seemed to do anything with them except kill each other.

There was to have been a joint Wehrmacht/IRA invasion of Northern Ireland, code-named "Operation Kathleen." According to the plan, the Germans were to land paratroops in two strategic locations; after the paratroops had landed, the IRA was to have invaded from the south. Following these initial actions, the Wehrmacht would send amphibious troops ashore and link up with the paratroops and the IRA.

The plan wasn't a bad one, and if Northern Ireland had been occupied, the Luftwaffe would have had bases close to the trans-Atlantic convoy routes. Bombers would then have been able to harass British and American shipping coming into Liverpool, and would also have been able to range far out to sea, to work with the U-Boats. The bomber fleets would have been in a better position to attack cities in the west of England, including Liverpool. Irish ports could also have been used as submarine bases—an even more strategic location than the Biscay ports of Brest and St. Nazaire.

Adolf Hitler himself took a personal interest in "Operation Kathleen." Admiral Canaris' harried man in Ireland, Hermann Goertz, was instructed to do everything possible to help the Irish Republican Army in carrying out its part of the operation.

But the IRA members decided they didn't want to carry out their end. A high-ranking officer leaked details about "Operation Kathleen" to the police, which effectively killed the invasion. Members of the IRA who were to have taken part in the offensive were arrested. The British Army was alerted and put additional men at strategic points in Northern Ireland. As soon as the Abwehr got wind of what was happening, the invasion and occupation of Northern Ireland was canceled.

Apparently, the IRA saw the invasion as too time-consuming and more in the interests of the German High Command than its own. So the IRA collected all the weapons and explosives it could get from the Germans, and then scuttled the operation. The IRA never could be counted on for any large-scale support; its actions in "Operation Kathleen" only confirmed this.

The Irish Republican Army could have been one of Germany's most effective allies, and one of the Allies' most dangerous enemies. It had the men, the organization, the weapons, and a thorough knowledge of guerrilla warfare.

What it lacked, in the German view, was discipline. Members had no desire to learn any new methods that might help them cooperate more closely with the Abwehr. Irish contacts would not even learn the most elementary of codes; all messages between Germany and the IRA had to be sent "in clear." "You're willing to die for Ireland," one exasperated German shouted at an IRA group, "but you haven't the slightest idea of how to fight for it."

The Republicans were also far more interested in fighting each other than in doing any real damage to the Allied war effort. Berlin assured the IRA that Northern Ireland would become united with the Irish Republic if Germany won the war, but this did not seem to inspire IRA members to fight for the German cause. Infighting within the IRA was so deeply ingrained that it could not be stopped for any reason, even a logical one.

148

A leading member of the IRA named Stephen Hayes was kidnapped and tortured by members of his own organization; he was suspected of disloyalty. Hayes was supposed to be the contact and liaison man for Hermann Goertz, who had parachuted into Ireland in May 1940. But after he managed to escape from his kidnappers, Hayes turned himself over to the police. He was afraid that he would be found again and the IRA would kill him if they ever got their hands on him a second time.

After he went to the police, Hayes began working for the Allies. Instead of going to the German Legation in Dublin with the messages Goertz gave him, Hayes went to MI.5, who turned Hayes into an agent for British Military Intelligence. So, in this one instance, the IRA actually performed a service for London.

It was lucky for MI.5 that the IRA didn't know how to fight for Ireland—and it was lucky for the FBI, since the Irish were active in the United States as well. Neither organization had the slightest idea of how to fight the IRA.

CHAPTER 11

More U-Boats and Cover-Ups

• • • • •

NOBODY KNOWS HOW MANY GERMAN AGENTS WERE AT WORK IN BRITAIN during World War II, whether affiliated with the Abwehr, the SS, or the IRA. Nobody has any idea how many German agents were at work in the United States, either, including "sleeper agents"; "good Germans," such as the man who smuggled plans for the Norden bombsight out of the country; and agents who came ashore from submarines. Neither MI.5 nor the FBI will admit that *any* spies or saboteurs even existed, let alone did any damage.

Several other landings via U-Boat were made in the United States, in addition to Operation Pastorius. Some were discovered; others were not.

On the night of April 13, 1942, the destroyer USS *Roper* encountered the submarine *U-85* running on the surface off the North Carolina coast. The usual procedure for a U-Boat in this situation is to pull the cork—to crash-dive. But *U-85* remained on the surface and was sunk by the *Roper*'s gunfire. No one could understand why the U-Boat had not submerged and attempted to escape.

The reason for this strange behavior became clear when bodies from the submarine were recovered. Some of the Germans were wearing civilian clothes; their billfolds held American currency, lots of it, as well as U.S. Social Security cards and other documents. *U-85* had been launching a rubber raft when the *Roper* discovered her. The destroyer had broken up an attempt to land German spies on the American mainland.

The would-be spies, as well as members of *U-85*'s crew, were buried in secret at the military cemetery in Hampton, Virginia.

It was a lucky find by the *Roper*; other similar attempts were not discovered. The last successful landing from a U-Boat, at least as far as anybody knows, took place at the end of 1944. Two men came ashore on the coast of Maine, two men who had almost nothing at all in common. One was a German, Erich Gimpel. The other was an American, William Colepaugh.

William Colepaugh was born in Connecticut in 1918, attended Admiral Farragut Academy in Toms Rover, New Jersey, and flunked out of Massachusetts Institute of Technology. His mother had been born in Germany; because of her influence, he identified more with Germany than with the United States, even though he did not speak a word of the German language.

Colepaugh did not set out to be a spy. His accidental career in espionage began when the German freighter *Pauline Frederik* docked in Boston harbor in the summer of 1939, and he became friendly with the crew. Colepaugh was a member of the U.S. Naval Reserve. He and the German sailors hung out in the same bars, where "there was a good deal of camaraderie and a great deal of whiskey."

The German sailors genuinely liked Colepaugh. They bought him drinks and called him "Wilhelm"—which he relished. He was invited to the captain's birthday party, where he met the German consul in Boston, Dr. Herbert Scholz.

Colepaugh has been described as "an accomplished drinker," as well as "easily influenced." Dr. Scholz was a persuasive propagandist and really poured it all over the easily influenced young Wilhelm. With no trouble at all, he convinced Colepaugh to go to work for the good of Greater Germany and that the Third Reich was going to win the war.

As part of his duties in the Naval Reserve, Colepaugh was required to complete a cruise. In May 1941, he sailed as part of a convoy to the British Isles. When Dr. Scholz found out about young Wilhelm's planned activities, he asked if Colepaugh would mind doing some spying for him—bringing back details on how the convoy operated and how the naval escort was deployed. The submarine campaign was just gathering strength, and U-Boat command wanted information on the destroyer screens that sailed with each convoy.

Colepaugh jumped at the chance. When his cruise ended in July, Colepaugh came back with up-to-date reports on Atlantic convoys: how destroyers guarded the flanks, air patrols, and other useful information. But Dr. Scholz was not around to send this data on to Berlin. He had been sent back to Germany—all German consulates had been closed by the increasing chill between Germany and the United States.

To add to his frustration, Colepaugh was refused a commission in the Naval Reserve. He was told that he was much too sympathetic toward Nazi Germany. Not only did his career in espionage seem to be over, but his naval career had definitely come to an abrupt end as well.

Colepaugh tried to get to Germany, without success. So he joined the Merchant Navy and sailed to Argentina. In Buenos Aires, he presented himself at the German Embassy, and asked permission to join the German army. But the Embassy staff told him that they had no means of getting him to Germany, which precluded his joining the Wehrmacht.

After making his way back to the United States, Colepaugh joined the U.S. Navy. But in 1943, he was released from the Navy, with an honorable discharge—again, because of his pro-German sympathies.

When he left the Navy, Colepaugh sailed to Portugal; he still had his heart set on getting into Germany and thought that someone in the German Embassy might be able to help him. In Lisbon, he presented himself at the embassy and used Dr. Scholz's name as a reference. The embassy staff, slightly taken aback by his request to enter Germany and more than a little suspicious, politely sent him away. But the embassy also notified Berlin of the fact that a strange American had asked to join the Wehrmacht and had mentioned Dr. Scholz.

When Dr. Scholz heard the story, he cabled Lisbon to keep an eye on Colepaugh, since he might be useful. Colepaugh had disappeared by that time, but he was located a short while later in a waterfront bar. Within a few days, he was on his way to Germany, at long last.

Colepaugh was given a thorough going-over by SS interrogators. They did not trust him very much and kept going over his story again and again. Why did he want to join the German Army? Why did he leave the United States? What were his feelings on the Nazi regime and Adolf Hitler? Also, Dr. Scholz was interviewed, along with any members of the *Pauline Frederick's* crew who could be found.

Finally, after many hours of interviews and interrogation, the SS decided that Colepaugh really was what he said he was—an American who was fed up with the United States and infatuated by Nazi Germany. He was just the opposite of George Dasch: a native-born German who couldn't stand Nazi Germany and wanted to help the American cause. As it turned out, Colepaugh would get a better deal from the Americans, in spite of his treachery, than George Dasch.

The SS may have believed Colepaugh's story, finally, but still didn't know what to do with him. He would be of no use in the Waffen SS—he was certainly no soldier, and anyway he neither spoke nor understood German. But as a native-born American, he might be useful for an espionage or sabotage assignment in the United States.

Colepaugh was interviewed by SS Major Otto Skorzeny, the man who led the operation to rescue Italian dictator Benito Mussolini from his mountain captivity in the Apennines. Mussolini's captors thought their prison was unassailable, but Skorzeny plucked the dictator off the mountain and delivered him to safety.

Skorzeny decided that Colepaugh would be best suited for the SD (Sicherheitsdienst), the SS intelligence branch. In 1944, the SD supplanted the Abwehr; Admiral Canaris was placed under arrest and replaced by SS Brigadier General Walter Schellenberg.

Once he was recruited into the SD, Colepaugh was sent to the espionage and sabotage school at Park Zorgvleit, near the Hague. Here, he would be trained for his upcoming assignment.

Erich Gimpel became a professional spy by degrees. He had been enlisted as an amateur spy by the German consulate in Lima, Peru, where he worked as a radio engineer in the 1930s. Although he had been born in Germany, Gimpel wanted to do some traveling; in South America, he would be well paid for his efforts.

The German minister in Lima put Gimpel to work watching ships in the harbor and reporting on their movements. He made reports on the usual details: date of arrival; cargo; nationality; name of captain; date of departure.

Gimpel kept up his activities for several years, from 1935 until 1942. He sent his reports to Chile via short wave; a contact in Chile relayed them to Germany. After war broke out between Germany and the United States, two American acquaintances got wise to Gimpel and reported him to their superiors. Word eventually reached the United States; the U.S. government put pressure on Peru to arrest Gimpel. In 1942, he was arrested and deported to Germany.

Back in Germany, he was sent for by the Abwehr, at 80 Tirpitz Ufer. The Abwehr knew all about his activities in Lima and had other things in mind for him. But before sending him off on another assignment, he was given formal training in espionage— methods of observation, shaking a pursuer, and other useful skills. These would not only help Gimpel do a better job, but would also help him to last longer while doing it.

After finishing his "spy course," Gimpel was sent off to Spain. The Abwehr wanted to get hold of some technical information on British radar development in that country. He had been given some technical training and, having lived in Peru for several years, spoke Spanish. Gimpel carried off his part of the assignment but, in spite of his efforts, the attempt to get hold of British radar secrets was only partially successful.

When he returned to Germany in 1943, Gimpel was told to organize an attempt to blow up the Panama Canal: "Operation Pelican." As far as Gimpel was concerned, this was a crazy idea; he had no faith at all in its success. His opinion was ignored by his superiors but, as it turned out, it didn't matter, anyway. "Operation Pelican" was called off before it got past the planning stage.

Following this, Gimpel was given another unusual job. Instead of being sent back to South America to keep track of Allied shipping, he would be sent to the United States to report on American progress in the field of nuclear energy.

Germany knew that the Americans had begun work on an atomic bomb but did not know how far the Manhattan Project had progressed. Gimpel spoke English and would be given all the assistance he would need to do the job; the Abwehr certainly had enough German-speaking friends in the United States to give all the help that might be needed.

But Gimpel had never been to the United States before. He was totally unfamiliar with the country, its people, and its customs. Also, Gimpel's knowledge of English was confined to the high school variety; and even this Germanic version of the "King's English" he spoke with an accent. His superiors in Berlin decided he should be given an American-speaking assistant, someone who spoke the language and knew something about the country and how its people lived. They managed to come up with the perfect candidate—somebody who not only knew about the United States, but had been born there and grew up there.

When Erich Gimpel first met William Colepaugh at the Park Zorgvliet estate he did not think very much of him. He always referred to Colepaugh as "Billy," as though the American were a little boy. This is exactly how Gimpel thought of him—an empty-headed, easily influenced, unreliable child.

The Abwehr officers in Berlin seemed to trust Colepaugh completely. Gimpel didn't. He could see that Billy was hardly a rock of stability; in a crisis, he would probably be totally useless. Also, he did not speak German, although this would not matter once they reached America. He wasn't exactly sure why he didn't trust Colepaugh, but a sixth sense told him that Billy should no be let out of his sight.

Gimpel and Colepaugh underwent training for their job in the United States at the Park Zorgvleit school. Much of it resembled the type of schedule that George Dasch and the others of Operation Pastorius had gone through. They practiced pistol shooting with both hands, they rode motorcycles, they handled explosives—none of which would have anything to do with their spy activities in the United States.

The useful part of their instruction involved the spotting and eluding of pursuers, which Gimpel had already learned, and sending messages in Morse code. Gimpel had already been trained in some of these things and had also practiced them in the field. Because of this prior experience, Gimpel's training lasted only four weeks; Colepaugh stayed for the entire eight weeks.

When their course at the Hague was over, they went to Berlin for more instruction. Gimpel arrived first, and Billy followed a few weeks later. They learned the basics of photography, using beautifully expensive Leica 35-millimeter cameras, as well as how to process negatives and make prints. Next, they were shown how to reduce the negatives to microdots.

Back in Berlin, the two were given their assignment. Besides finding out about the atomic bomb project, they were also to gather as much technical data as possible on American shipbuilding and aircraft manufacturing. Their principal sources of information would be articles in newspapers and technical magazines, radio broadcasts, and recent books—products of America's freedom of speech. Urgent information was to be radioed to Germany. Otherwise, articles were to be photographed, reduced to microdots, and air mailed to a cover address in a neutral country.

A great deal had been learned about American industry through articles in papers, such as *The New York Times*. But lately, information from the newspapers had been taking too long to cross the Atlantic. Gimpel and Colepaugh were to speed up the process.

Erich Gimpel's cover name was Edward Green; Colepaugh's was William Caldwell. They were issued with the same forged identity papers that George Dasch and all the other spies were given—birth certificates, draft cards, and driving licenses. They were also issued $60,000 in cash and Gimpel was given custody of 99 chip diamonds, to be sold in an emergency. Their assignment in the United States was to last two years; afterward, they would return to Germany.

At the end of September 1944, the two were ready to depart. They boarded the submarine *U-1230* in Kiel harbor. Allied forces had retaken Brittany since the D-Day landings in June; the ports of St. Nazaire and Lorient, the main bases for Admiral Dönitz's U-Boats, were now closed to the German Navy. Submarines now had a longer, and more perilous, trip—from German ports, the way into the Atlantic was around Denmark and into the mine-infested North Sea.

While on board the U-Boat, Gimpel and Colepaugh both wore naval uniforms. Gimpel looked the part he was playing. He was actually mistaken for a Chief engineer, which was his cover, and was even buttonholed by three U-Boat commanders with technical questions about radar.

Billy was supposed to be a war correspondent, complete with camera dangling from neck strap, but nobody was fooled by his cover for a minute. He spoke no German, handled a camera as though he had never seen one before, and acted more like a schoolboy than a reporter. During the crossing, the favorite topic among the crew was the identity of the two strangers on board.

The crew certainly had enough time to speculate—the crossing took 46 days. British and American sound-detecting devices made traveling at high speed unsafe, if not absolutely suicidal. *U-1230* was one of the big, new Type IX-C subs, built by Deutche Werk at Hamburg and launched in November 1943. She was capable of 7.25 knots submerged and over 18 knots on the surface. But *U-1230* crept across the Atlantic at 2 knots—about 50 miles per day.

Throughout the journey, by order of the captain, Leutnant Hilbig, *U-1230* remained submerged. Only once did the boat surface, and that was because of an emergency—toxic diesel exhaust overcame some of the crew, and a dose of fresh air became necessary. Otherwise, it was seven and one half weeks of cramped quarters, foul air, taut nerves, and tension. Because of enemy sound detectors, nobody was even allowed to speak above a whisper.

When the U-Boat was still four days away from its destination, Frenchman's Bay on the Maine coast, Hilbig received a radio signal: "The enemy may be apprised of our undertaking. Act according to your own discretion."

Gimpel and Hilbig studied coastal charts to find another place to land, but every place that looked safe was too shallow. Finally, Gimpel decided to land at Frenchman's Bay and take his chances. It was either that or turn back for Kiel.

A U.S. Navy destroyer was on patrol in the bay; the U-Boat crew could hear its screws. But the destroyer apparently had its listening apparatus turned off, as well as its radar. The coast watchers were also less than alert; they didn't see anything. "If the American coast defenses had not been asleep," Gimpel pointed out, "we should have been discovered long since."

On November 29, Gimpel and Colepaugh changed from uniforms into civilian clothes. When it was dark, the U-Boat surfaced. After watching a car drive past on the shore, close enough for the driver to have seen *U-1230,* Gimpel and Colepaugh dropped into a rubber dinghy and were rowed to shore by crew members. They scrambled onto the beach, each man carrying a suitcase and a loaded revolver.

As soon as the crew of the dinghy got back to the U-Boat, Hilbig headed for the safety of the open sea.

While Gimpel and Colepaugh were still on the sub, it had started snowing. They walked through some woods to a dirt road and were passed by a car. Eventually, they reached the main highway, U.S. 1 and were picked up by a taxi, which took them to the rail station in Bangor. From Bangor, they took a train to Portland; from Portland, they went by train to Boston, and then on to New York.

They had two close calls already, although they didn't know it. The first one took place while they were on the dirt road, on their way to highway U.S. 1. The driver of the car that had passed them was suspicious of the two men—they were carrying suitcases, which was unusual enough by itself, but were also wearing only light topcoats and no hats. Nobody who lived in Maine would wear such a light coat in November, nor would they go bareheaded in a snowstorm.

The driver, a high school senior named Hodgkins, decided to investigate. He went back to the dirt road and traced the two sets of footprints in the snow back to the water's edge—*U-1230* had long since vanished. There had been warnings of spies in the area, so he drove home to report the incident to his father. His father was a deputy sheriff of the county.

But by the time the elder Hodgkins arrived at the scene, the snow had turned to rain and had washed away the footprints of Gimpel and Colepaugh. Since the evidence had disappeared, Deputy Sheriff Hodgkins let the matter drop.

The second close call did not directly involve Gimpel and Colepaugh. It was triggered by Lt. Hilbig, the captain of *U-1230*.

After Hilbig took *U-1230* out of Frenchman's Bay, he thought it best to lay low for a while. The boat was kept submerged at all times, day and night, and on the ocean bottom for long stretches. Traveling was done only for short intervals, and at very slow speed. He had pressed his luck by coming right into Frenchman's Bay, within sight of land, and had got away with it. He did not want to tempt the fates, or the U.S. coastal patrols, again.

On the morning of December 8, 1944, the submarine was still only a short distance away from the coast. A British freighter, heading north on its way to St. John's, Newfoundland, was detected by the U-Boat's listening apparatus. Lt. Hilbig's love for the hunt got the better of his instinct for survival. He brought *U-1230* up to periscope depth and, in the early brightness, torpedoed the 5,000-ton *Cornwallis*, which sank in 10 minutes. Following this welcome break in the monotony, *U-1230* once again disappeared.

The *Cornwallis* was the first ship to be torpedoed off the American coast in quite some time. The U.S. Coast Guard doubted that a German submarine would venture so close to shore just to sink one small British merchantman. There was very probably some other reason for the U-Boat's presence in that particular area.

The eight men of Operation Pastorius had been landed by submarines, it was recalled. There had also been several other failed attempts to land spies by U-Boat, including one during the preceding autumn, and probably many undetected attempts, as well. The *Cornwallis* incident had all the markings of another landing—the U-Boat probably picked off the freighter after dropping its passengers. The FBI was informed, and the bureau began an investigation.

Federal agents began interviewing residents along the Maine coast. When they spoke with young Hodgkins, they realized that they were on to something and intensified their efforts. But nobody else in the Frenchman's Bay area—bus drivers, truck drivers, train conductors—noticed anyone foreign-looking or suspicious. The FBI didn't bother talking to taxi drivers.

Erich Gimpel and Billy Colepaugh couldn't believe that the FBI hadn't found out about them. They had traveled all the way to Manhattan without anyone so much as raising an eyebrow in their direction.

Gimpel's mind was on his assignment. He bought the parts for a short wave radio—separately, so that no one would suspect anything—and built it himself. He rented a flat for Billy and himself, where they would be much less conspicuous than if they stayed in a hotel. And, the most difficult part, he kept an eye on Billy.

Billy's main concern was spending money, picking up girls, and having a good time. He was spending at the rate of about $500 per day—in 1944, $500 was about three months' wages in the United States—mostly on drink and night clubs. Gimpel worried that this free-spending would attract attention. He tried to reason with Billy, with no luck. Colepaugh was more interested in visiting restaurants and nightclubs than in sending reports to Germany.

After a few weeks in New York, Colepaugh was tired of playing spy, even though he hadn't even begun playing yet, and became generally depressed—"an attack of the miseries," Gimpel called it. It could have been triggered by a number of things: war nerves, too much drink, Gimpel's scolding, or any combination of the three. Billy was not very trustworthy under the best of circumstances. In his present state of mind, he would be capable of doing anything.

One day when Gimpel was out of the flat, Colepaugh decided to take all their money and disappear. He took the two suitcases—containing Gimpel's radio transmitter and almost $60,000 in cash, along with the chip diamonds—and left the flat.

On his way out, he explained to his landlady that he was going to Connecticut, to spend Christmas with some relatives. After wishing his landlady a merry Christmas, Colepaugh took a taxi to Grand Central Station, the rail link between Manhattan and the northern areas, where he left the two suitcases in the baggage room. Then he went off into the crowd, probably for another round of drinking.

When Gimpel returned to the flat and saw the suitcases gone, he knew at once what had happened—Billy was hard to control, but easy to figure. The landlady obligingly told him that Colepaugh had gone off to Connecticut for Christmas. He managed to trace Billy to Grand Central Station by asking various newsboys and doormen. "The trail of a man who walks through New York in broad daylight carrying two large suitcases is not all that difficult to follow," Gimpel admitted.

At Grand Central, he spotted the two suitcases through the door of the baggage office. Although he didn't have the claim ticket, Gimpel did have the keys to open the cases—Colepaugh apparently planned to break the locks when he got to Connecticut.

Gimpel explained to the baggage room clerk that the suitcases were his, but that he had lost the ticket. To convince the clerk, Gimpel described the contents of one of the bags—the one without the money and radio—and proceeded to open it with his keys. Inside were the clothes, socks, underwear and Leica camera, just as Gimpel had said.

The plan worked—Gimpel had convinced the clerk that he owned the bags. Gimpel signed the receipt, using his cover name, Edward Green, and left the rail station before the clerk had a chance to change his mind.

The situation between Gimpel and Colepaugh was now reversed—Gimpel now had all the money, while Billy was out in the cold in New York. He still had several thousand dollars in his pocket, but that would not last Billy very long.

Colepaugh was now on his own and had no idea what to do. He was not used to being alone, and New York is not the friendliest city on earth under the best of circumstances. Had he been level-headed, he could have figured some way out of his predicament. But had he been level-headed, he would not have been Billy Colepaugh.

When he realized that Gimpel had turned the tables on him, as soon as he tried to collect his bags at Grand Central, he reacted in a typical way—by going off on a drunk. After two days of it, he went to visit an old acquaintance named Edward Mulcahy. (Gimpel gives the name as Tom S. Warrens.)

Gimpel had not given any thought to what Billy would do when he was left alone, with no one to take him by the hand. He should have realized that Colepaugh would turn to someone in whom he could "confide"—or, in less charitable terms, someone he could spill his guts to. Which is exactly what happened.

Whatever his friend's name, Mulcahy or Warrens, Colepaugh told him everything—about why he was in the United States, about Gimpel, about *U-1230*, about the spy school at the Hague. He also wanted advice on what he should do now—now that Gimpel had taken all the money and disappeared. Colepaugh's friend suggested that they contact the FBI; Colepaugh agreed. But before they did anything else, they decided to go out and have a drink.

Warrens/Mulcahy was a man after Colepaugh's heart. Billy arrived at his flat to talk on December 23. The two of them kept drinking, going to parties, and talking about the FBI until the day after Christmas. On December 26, Warrens/Mulcahy finally telephoned the federal agents.

A special agent came to the flat to talk to Colepaugh. Billy had an easier time communicating with the FBI than George Dasch. After examining the evidence—some microdots, $1,999 in cash, a German watch, and some false identification papers—the agent took Colepaugh to headquarters for a more thorough questioning.

At FBI headquarters, Colepaugh told his interrogators everything they wanted to know about the spy operation, as well as about Erich Gimpel, alias Edward Green. His description of Gimpel was very detailed, even down to Gimpel's habit of keeping his change in the left breast pocket of his jacket.

There were several reasons behind Colepaugh's actions. First, he didn't have the nerve to go through with the assignment—or the short-wave radio. Also he was afraid of what might happen to him if he did go through with it—he was probably as afraid of succeeding as he was of failing. It has been suggested that Hitler's "Battle of the Bulge" offensive in December 1944, in which American forces took a terrible beating for over a week, was partly responsible—he apparently wanted Germany to win the war, but he did not want America to lose it.

But the main reason was that he was alone, with his money supply gone, as well as Gimpel, his headmaster. Colepaugh had nowhere else to turn, so he turned to the FBI. Gimpel hadn't thought of this when he took the two suitcases from Grand Central's baggage room.

With the information and description of Gimpel given by Colepaugh, federal agents didn't have much trouble finding Billy's partner. On December 30, FBI agents saw a man who answered Gimpel's description in Times Square. The man was buying a South American newspaper. When he paid for it, he was given change; he put the change in his left breast pocket. The G-men knew they had their man.

The FBI's version of the capture and arrest of Erich Gimpel and William Colepaugh is, astonishingly enough, not very different from Gimpel's version. The FBI never tried to cover the fact that it owed its success to Colepaugh's information—if he hadn't given himself up, the pair probably would not have been discovered before the war ended.

J. Edgar Hoover's uncharacteristic generosity probably has a lot to do with the war being almost over by the time Gimpel and Colepaugh landed in Maine. Even if the two had completed their assignment, it wouldn't have mattered. Besides, Hoover had deluged the American public with so many glittering stories of FBI successes that by 1945, even *he* was satisfied. That is, if it is possible for an ego the size of Hoover's ever to be satisfied.

The fact that the bureau's investigation in Maine was not as thorough as it should have been was not mentioned in any of the official accounts, but this is to be expected. By not questioning taxi operators in the Frenchman's Bay area, the FBI allowed the two spies to get away—information that did not come to light until over 30 years after the war ended.

Another difference between the FBI's version of events and Gimpel's involved America's top secret atomic energy program, the "Manhattan Project."

Gimpel claims that one of his objectives was to find out everything possible about the Manhattan Project. German Intelligence knew about America's atomic bomb, but did not know how far the building of the bomb had progressed. Gimpel was to find out. The FBI does not mention this.

Gimpel also claims that he succeeded in learning that the Manhattan Project had produced "two or three" of the bombs, and that they would be ready by mid-1945, along with "a mass of technical details." He also claims to have sent a report to Germany about these details, a report which took "8 to 10 minutes" to send. The FBI certainly does not mention this, either.

Of course, Gimpel may have been making up this part of the story; he wouldn't have been the first spy to embellish his activities to make them seem more colorful. Colepaugh did not seem to know anything about the atomic part of the assignment, but this doesn't prove anything. It is more than possible that Gimpel didn't tell Billy anything that was not absolutely necessary. His mistrust of Billy, as it turned out, was well founded.

But J. Edgar Hoover certainly would not have been above keeping this part of the story from the public. Hoover was extremely sensitive about the security that surrounded the Manhattan Project, even though it was not solely the responsibility of the FBI; military counterintelligence also played a large role in guarding the atomic secrets. "The Best-Kept Secret of the War" was an achievement that Hoover liked to boast about.

Hoover always covered up any information relating to any successful spy operations in the United States. He would certainly have made a special effort to bury the story of a successful attempt to send atomic secrets to Germany, even at that late stage of the war. And he had the power and the influence to kill any story or news release he decided was objectionable, or that hurt the bureau's image.

Both Erich Gimpel and William Colepaugh were tried for espionage, found guilty, and sentenced to death by hanging. The sentence was to have been carried out within four days. But the day before Gimpel was to be hanged, President Franklin D. Roosevelt died from a cerebral hemorrhage. Which meant four weeks' state mourning, during which no death sentences could be carried out.

Before the mourning period ended, Germany surrendered. With the European war over, Roosevelt's successor, Harry S. Truman, commuted Gimpel's sentence to life imprisonment.

Gimpel spent the next nine years of his life in American prisons, before being pardoned and deported to Germany. While he was serving time in Leavenworth Penitentiary, he met George Dasch.

Dasch's treatment on the "inside" was no better than it had been at the hands of the military judicial system. He was considered a traitor by the other inmates and was given the "silent treatment"—shunned by prison society, a punishment reserved for individuals who give evidence against their partners in crime. One of the prisoners even approached Gimpel with an unusual offer—he would kill Dasch, making it look like an accident, if Gimpel would give him 10 packs of cigarettes.

Desirability and Appearance

$\bullet \quad \bullet \quad \bullet \quad \bullet \quad \bullet$

IN THE MID-1980S, A BRITISH WRITER TOOK A TRIP TO EASTERN LONG ISLAND to gather material for a still-unformed book. Or, as he puts it, "to look for a novel." He rented a house near the town of Sag Harbor, 86 miles from New York City, and began looking.

Several weeks later, he was still looking. "I accumulated a great wealth of background," our novelist said. "But no plot."

Toward the end of summer, he attended a breakfast barbecue at the Sag Harbor fire house. A member of the police force, the "benign local cop," was also there. The conversation turned toward the policeman's service revolver, and if he would soon be getting a new one.

"The gun I have dates from 1942," the policeman said, "the time the Nazi spies landed." After listening to what the policeman had to say about the incident, the novelist decided that the "Nazi spies" was the story he had been looking for. He had finally found his novel.

His first step in researching his novel would be to find out all that he could about the German "spies." Interviews did not help very much; the landing had taken place over 40 years earlier, and most people did not remember it. Those who did remember seemed embarrassed by the incident and were reluctant to talk about it.

Having failed to learn anything from the locals, the next move was to look in the public records. The visitor from Britain discovered a file on the "Pastorius Case" in Washington, D.C.—in the archives of the Federal Bureau of Investigation. He spent much of his remaining time in the United States poring over the FBI's version of the account—all 13,984 pages of it.

Our author wrote his novel, based on the landing from *U-202*, which was published in the 1980s. He also wrote an article for the newspaper supplement *You*, which he called "Hitler's American Beach Party." Not surprisingly, the article strictly follows the FBI's version of the story and does not even hint that there might be another side to it.

According to the article, George Dasch was a "double-traitor," who gave up his fellow saboteurs to save his own life; Coast-guardsman John Cullen was a hero who "sounded the alarm"; the military trial was nothing out of the ordinary; and George Dasch's secret deportation to Germany was exactly what he deserved. J. Edgar Hoover's role in the proceedings was not mentioned—his presence was everywhere, but never seen. Which was the way Hoover planned it.

In other words, the British novelist believed every word of the FBI's account. From the information he read, how could he have done otherwise?

By the late 1980s, Hoover and the bureau had been flooding the media with the FBI's own version for nearly half a century—newspapers, books, magazines, and even television shows in the 1950s and 1960s. Details that might put the bureau in a bad light—such as events surrounding the trial and deportation of George Dasch—were never mentioned, or even hinted at. Most of these magazine articles and television programs were written with the "technical assistance" of the bureau. Official records made no mention of these details either, of course, and played down Dasch's central role in the capture of the Pastorius saboteurs. The only version of the Pastorius story that is not based upon FBI files is George Dasch's own account, *Eight Spies Against America*, which was published by a small press and received little notice.

According to official FBI statistics, 19,649 cases of suspected sabotage were investigated during the war; not one of these cases was the work of enemy agents. The bureau insists that its record against spies and saboteurs was perfect, and it manufactured its own statistics to prove it.

In newspaper and magazine articles, as well as in personal speeches and addresses, Hoover himself made the same assertion. He spoke and wrote about the FBI's "prevention" of sabotage and espionage, and insisted that enemy activity in the United States had been "kept under control." No "military secrets" had ever been smuggled out of the country, Hoover insisted, maintaining that all saboteurs had been rounded up and rendered harmless.

Which means Hermann Lang did not smuggle the secret plans for the Norden bomb sight across to Germany; that German-American Bund members and pro-Nazi sympathizers did not slow production in several factories during the war; and that the mysterious fires and explosions reported by Hartford Insurance were a figment of somebody's imagination.

Although this has been the official FBI line since the war, the bureau *has* admitted that spies loyal to the Soviet Union were active in the United States all throughout the war. Although there were no German spies in the country (or Japanese), there were Communists all over the place, gathering information on American "military secrets" and sending it off to Moscow. Nobody in the bureau has been able to explain this oddity—why the FBI was able to capture all German spies, but could not keep the Russians "under control." Apparently it was easier to capture and neutralize a Nazi agent than a Communist.

British counterintelligence is just as emphatic about its record against German agents, although not quite as blatant as Hoover. Officially, both Scotland Yard and MI.5 deny that any act of sabotage or espionage had taken place in Britain during the war, or that any enemy agent had been at large. Like the FBI, they insisted—and continue to insist—that "industrial accidents" were the cause of all "undetermined" explosions. Incidents that could not be explained away, such as the IRA bombing of Hammersmith Bridge in 1939, were simply ignored—no explanation was even attempted.

In *The Devil's Dictionary*, Ambrose Bierce defined "Truth" as, "An ingenious compound of desirability and appearance." This certainly seems to fit the FBI's definition, along with that of British Intelligence. Both agencies seemed to have been far more concerned with appearances than with facts. (J. Edgar Hoover was obsessed with appearances.) And desirability ran a close second—they worked with single-minded determination to convince the public that their myth of invincibility was actually fact. (It can be argued that Hoover worked harder at publicity than at apprehending spies and saboteurs.)

Even decades after World War II had ended, neither the FBI nor MI.5 (or Scotland Yard) will admit that enemy agents were active in their respective countries both before and during the war. They would certainly not ever admit that enormous assistance was rendered to the Nazi cause. Their brand of truth does not allow for facts, only for appearances and desirability.

APPENDIX

The "Official" FBI Version of German Sabotage Operations in the United States

• • • • •

A CCORDING TO THIS ACCOUNT, GEORGE DASCH WENT TO THE FBI ABOUT OPER-ation Pastorius "to protect himself"—to turn the others in before somebody else got the same idea and turned *him* in. But none of the Pastorius defendants, except Dasch and Burger, mentioned any desire to warn the FBI of the sabotage operation. It is nothing more than a statement to discredit Dasch, an attempt to make him seem a coward as well as a traitor. (Burger's motives are never mentioned.)

George Dasch is not even mentioned by name in the encounter with Coastguardsman John C. Cullen. The FBI account says, "They offered him a bribe to forget they had met." This is a deliberate distortion of events. Of the four men from *U-202*, only Dasch approached Cullen and spoke to him. His intent was to send Cullen away before any harm could come to him, as well as to arouse the coastguardsman's suspicions—not "to forget they had met."

Neither Attorney General Francis Biddle nor J. Edgar Hoover ever "appealed to President Roosevelt" to commute the sentences of Dasch and Burger. In fact, Hoover was not at all happy when he learned that Dasch and Burger were not to be executed. If it had been left up to him, both would have gone to the electric chair, along with the other six Pastorius defendants.

The landing of William Colepaugh and Erich Gimpel is given a glossing over in this account, with many essential details deliberately left out. The two certainly were "quickly apprehended by the FBI." Their quick apprehension took place because William Colepaugh went to the FBI and turned himself in, along with Erich Gimpel—a fact that is conveniently omitted.

The pardoning and deportation of Dasch and Burger is made to appear as a humane act. In fact, the two were hurried out of the country before anyone could find out about it. Even George Dasch's American wife was not informed that her husband had been released from prison and was being sent to Germany.

The statements, "no similar sabotage attempt was ever again made" and "no other attempt was made to land saboteurs by submarine," are nothing but lies. At least one other attempt was made, in April 1942, when the submarine *U-85* had already begun preparations for landing a party of Germans on the coast of North Carolina. This particular landing was broken up by the chance encounter with the destroyer USS *Roper*, which sank the U-Boat with gunfire. Similar attempts by other U-Boats were not discovered.

Another outright lie is the statement that "not one instance was found of enemy-inspired sabotage." The Abwehr had its members installed in a number of important factories and installations, including the Liquidometer plant in New York and in Brewster Aeronautical—32 of them were discovered in the Brewster plant alone. Hoover knew all about them—he just refused to admit it to the public.

This account contains just enough fact to make it seem credible: biographical data about George Dasch and information about the date and time of the landings in Florida and on Long Island. But most of it is a combination of lies, half-truths, and distortions.

RE: George John Dasch, and the Nazi Saboteurs Revised March 1984

Shortly after midnight on the morning of June 13, 1942, four men landed on a beach near Amagansett, Long Island, from a German submarine, clad in German uniforms and bringing ashore enough explosives, primers, and incendiaries to support an expected two-year career in the sabotage of American defense-related production. On June 17, 1942, a similar group landed on Ponte Vedra Beach, near Jacksonville, Florida, equipped for a similar career in industrial disruption.

The purpose of the invasions was to strike a major blow for Germany by bringing the violence of war to our home ground through destruction of America's ability to manufacture vital equipment and supplies and transport them to the battlegrounds of Europe, to strike fear into the American civilian population, and diminish the resolve of the United States to overcome our enemies.

By June 17, 1942, all eight saboteurs had been arrested without having accomplished one act of destruction. Tried before a military commission, they were found guilty. One was sentenced to life imprisonment, another to 30 years, and 6 received the death penalty, which was carried out within a few days.

The magnitude of the euphoric expectation of the Nazi war machine may be judged by the fact that, in addition to the large amount of material brought ashore by the saboteurs, they were given $175,200 in United States currency to finance their activities. On apprehension, a total of $174,588 was recovered by the FBI—the only positive accomplishment of eight trained saboteurs in those two weeks was the expenditure of $612 for clothing, meals, lodging and travel, and a bribe of $260.

So shaken was the German intelligence service that no similar sabotage attempt was ever again made. The German Naval High Command did not again allow a valuable submarine to be risked for a sabotage mission.

On September 1, 1939, World War II opened in Europe with the invasion of Poland by Nazi Germany. The United States remained neutral until drawn into the world conflict by the Japanese attack on Pearl Harbor on December 7, 1941. War was declared against Japan by the United States on December 8, 1941, and, on December 11, Germany and Italy declared war against the United States.

During the early months of the war, the major contributions of the United States to oppose the Nazi war machine involved industrial production, equipment and supplies furnished to those forces actively defending themselves against the German armed forces. That industrial effort was strong enough to generate frustration, perhaps indignation, among the Nazi High Command and the order was given, allegedly by Hitler himself, to mount a serious effort to reduce American production.

German Intelligence settled on sabotage as the most effective means of diminishing our input. In active charge of the project was Lieutenant Walter Kappe, attached to Abwehr-2 (Intelligence 2) who had spent some years in the United States prior to the war and had been active in the German-American Bund and other efforts in the U.S. to propagandize and win adherents for Nazism among German-Americans and German immigrants in America. Kappe was also an official of the Ausland Institute which, prior to the war, organized Germans abroad into the *Nationalsozialistiche Deutshe Arbeiterpartei*, the NSDAP or Nazi Party. During the conflict, Ausland kept track of and in touch with persons in Germany who had returned from abroad. Kappe's responsibility concerned those who had returned from the U.S.

Early in 1942, he contacted, among others, those who ultimately undertook the mission to the United States Each consented to the task, apparently willingly, although unaware of the specific assignment. Most of the potential saboteurs were taken from civilian jobs but two were in the German army.

The trainees, about twelve in all, were told of their specific mission only when they entered a sabotage school established near Berlin which instructed them in chemistry, incendiaries, explosives, timing devices, secret writing, and concealment of identity by blending into an American background. The intensive training included the practical use of the techniques under realistic conditions.

Subsequently, the saboteurs were taken to aluminum and magnesium plants, railroad shops, canals, locks, and other facilities to familiarize them with the vital points and vulnerabilities of the types of targets they were to attack. Maps were used to locate those American targets, spots where railroads could be most effectively disabled, the principal aluminum and magnesium plants, and important canals, waterways, and locks. All instructions had to be memorized.

On May 26, 1942, the first group of four saboteurs left by submarine from the German base at Lorient, France, and on May 28, the next group of four departed the same base. Each was destined to land at a point on the Atlantic Coast of the United States familiar to the leader of that group.

Four men, led by George John Dasch, age 39, landed on a beach near Amagansett, Long Island, New York, about 12:10 A.M., June 13, 1942. Accompanying Dasch were Ernest Peter Burger, 36; Heinrich Harm Heinck, 35; and Richard Quirlin, 34.

On June 17, 1942, the other group landed at Ponte Vedra Beach, Florida, south of Jacksonville. The leader was Edward John Kerling, age 33, with Werner Thiel, 35; Herman Otto Neubauer, 32; and Herbert Hans Haupt, 22. Both groups landed wearing complete or partial German uniforms to ensure treatment as prisoners of war, rather than as spies, if they were caught in the act of landing.

Having landed unobserved, the uniforms were quickly discarded, to be buried with the sabotage material (which was intended to be later retrieved) and civilian clothing was donned. The saboteurs quickly dispersed. The Florida group made its way to Jacksonville, then by train to Cincinnati, with two going on to Chicago and the other pair to New York City.

The Long Island group was less fortunate; scarcely had they buried their equipment and uniforms, in fact, one still wore bathing trunks, when a coast guardsman patrolling the shore approached. He was unarmed and very suspicious of them, more so when they offered him a bribe to forget they had met. He ostensibly accepted the bribe to lull their fears and promptly reported the incident to his headquarters. However, by the time the search patrol located the spot, the saboteurs had reached a railroad station and taken a train to New York City.

Dasch's resolution to be a saboteur for the Fatherland faltered—perhaps he thought the whole project so grandiose as to be impractical and wanted to protect himself before some of his companions took action on similar doubts. He indicated to Burger his desire to confess everything.

On the evening of June 14, 1942, Dasch, giving the name "Pastorius" called the New York office of the FBI, stating he had recently arrived from Germany and would call FBI headquarters when he was in Washington, D.C., the following week. On the morning of Friday, June 19, a call was received at the FBI in Washington from Dasch, then registered at a Washington hotel. He alluded to his prior call as "Pastorius" (of which headquarters was aware) and furnished his location. He was immediately contacted and taken into custody.

During the next several days he was thoroughly interrogated and he furnished the identities of the other saboteurs, possible locations for some, and data which would enable their more expeditious apprehension.

The three remaining members of the Long Island group were picked up in New York City on June 20. Of the Florida group, Kerling and Thiel were arrested in New York City on June 23, and Neubauer and Haupt in Chicago on June 27.

The eight were tried before a military commission, seven U.S. Army officers appointed by President Roosevelt, from July 8 to August 4, 1942. The trial was held in the Department of Justice Building, Washington, D.C. The prosecution was headed by Attorney General Frances Biddle and the Army judge advocate general, Major General Myron C. Cramer. Defense counsel included Colonel Kenneth C. Royal (later secretary of war under President Truman) and Major Lauren H. Stone (son of Harlan Fiske Stone, then chief justice of the U.S. Supreme Court).

All eight were found guilty and sentenced to death. Attorney General Biddle and J. Edgar Hoover appealed to President Roosevelt to commute the sentences of Dasch and Burger; Dasch then received a 30-year sentence, and Burger a life sentence, both to be served in a federal penitentiary. The remaining six were executed at the District of Columbia jail on August 8, 1942.

The eight men had been born in Germany and each had lived in the United States for substantial periods. Burger had become a naturalized American in 1933. Haupt had entered the United States as a child, gaining citizenship when his father was naturalized in 1930.

Dasch had joined the German army at the age of 14 and served about 11 months as a clerk during the conclusion of World War I. He had enlisted in the U.S. Army in 1927, and received an honorable discharge after a little more than a year of service.

Quirin and Heinck had returned to Germany prior to the outbreak of World War II in Europe, and the six others subsequent to September 1, 1939, and before December 7, 1941, apparently feeling their first loyalty was to the country of their birth.

Postwar debriefing of German personnel and examination of records confirmed that no other attempt was made to land saboteurs by submarine, though in late 1944, two persons, William Curtis Colepaugh and Erich Gimpel, were landed as spies from a German sub on the coast of Maine, in a rather desperate attempt to secure information. They, too, were quickly apprehended by the FBI before accomplishing any part of their mission.

In April 1948, President Truman granted executive clemency to Dasch and Burger on condition of deportation. They were transported to the American Zone of Germany, the unexecuted portions of their sentences were suspended upon such conditions with respect to travel, employment, political, and other activities as the theater commander might require, and they were freed.

As a footnote, although many allegations of sabotage were investigated by the FBI during World War II, not one instance was found of enemy-inspired sabotage. Every suspect act traced to its source was the result of vandalism, pique, resentment, a desire for relief from boredom, the curiosity of children "to see what would happen," or other personal motive.

Bibliography

Brown, Anthony Cave. *Bodyguard of Lies*. New York, Doubleday, 1975.

Carter, Carolle J. *The Shamrock and the Swastika*. Palo Alto, California: Pacific Books, 1979.

Chase, Allan, *Falange*. New York: G. P. Putnam, 1942.

Collins, GL. *The FBI in Peace and War*. New York, 1940.

Dasch, George. *Eight Spies Against America*. New York: Robert M. McBride Co., 1959.

Dönitz, Karl. *Memoirs: Ten Years and Twenty Days*. New York: World Publishing Co., 1959.

Farago, Ladislas. *The Game of the Foxes*. New York: Bantam Books, 1973

Gimpel, Erich. *Spy For Germany*. London: Robert Hale, 1959.

Hilton, Stanley E. *Hitler's Secret War in South America, 1939–1945*. Baton Rouge, Louisiana: Louisiana State University Press, 1981.

Hoover, J. Edgar. "The Spy Who Double-Crossed Hitler," in *American* magazine, May 1946.

Johnson, David. *V For Vengeance*. London: William Kimber, 1981.

Kahn, David. *Hitler's Spies*. London: Hodder & Stoughton, 1972.

Mosley, Leonard. *The Druid*. London: Eyre Methuen, 1982.

Newman, Bernard. *Spies in Britain*. London: Robert Hale, 1964.

Work of Espionage. London: World Distributors, 1962.

O'Callaghan, Sean. *The Jackboot in Ireland*. London: Allan Wingate, 1958.

Rachlis, Eugene. *They Came to Kill*. New York: Random House, 1961.

Stephan, Enno. *Spies in Ireland*. London: Macdonald, 1963.

Swanberg, W. A. "The Spies Who Came In From The Sea," in *American Heritage*, April 1970.

"The Day JFK's Father Captured a Top Nazi Spy," in *Stag* magazine, April 1963.

"The Untold Story of the Nazi Saboteurs," in *Newsweek*, November 12, 1945.

Turner, William. *Hoover's FBI: The Man and the Myth*. New York: Sherburne Press, 1970.

"Under the Cloak of Night," in U.S. Naval Institute Proceedings, June 1982.

Watters, editor. *Investigating the FBI*. New York: Doubleday, 1971.

Watts, Anthony J. *The U-Boat Hunters*. London: Macdonald & Jane's, 1976.

West, Nigel. *MI.5*. London: The Bodley Head, 1981.

Whitehous, Don. *The FBI Story*. New York, 1956.

Wiighton, Charles and Gunter Peis. *They Spied on England*. London: Odhams Press, 1958.

In addition, numerous editions of magazines from the years 1939–45, including *Time*, *Life*, *Look*, *Reader's Digest*, and *Newsweek*, were consulted. Local newspapers, especially the *New York Times* and some New Jersey papers, were also useful.

Index